The Complete Player:
A Brit and a Texan Navigate the Junior Tennis Journey

Tim Bainton & Jeremy Carl

The Complete Player:
A Brit and a Texan Navigate the Junior Tennis Journey

Copyright © 2018 Tim Bainton & Jeremy Carl
ALL RIGHTS RESERVED

No part of this publication may be reproduced, stored in or introduced into a retrieval system, or transmitted, in any form or by any means (electronically, mechanical, photocopying, recording or otherwise), without the prior written permission of both the copyright owners and the publisher of this book.

Re-selling through electronic outlets like (Amazon, Barnes & Noble or eBay) without permission of the publisher is illegal and punishable by law.

The scanning, uploading, and distribution of this book via the Internet or any other means without the permission of the publisher is illegal and punishable by law.

Please purchase only authorized editions and do not participate in or encourage electronic piracy of copyrighted materials.

Your support of the authors' right is appreciated.

ISBN-13: 978-1987432718   ISBN-10: 1987432711

COVER DESIGN AND LAYOUT: HELEN BAINTON

LIBRARY OF CONGRESS CATALOGING-IN-PUBLICATION DATA

Bainton, Tim and Carl, Jeremy
The Complete Player: A Brit and a Texan Navigate the Junior Tennis Journey
1. 2. 3. 4.
I. Title.

Also available by Tim Bainton and Jeremy Carl

The Complete Coach: A Brit and a Texan Solve the Coaching Puzzle
(Create Space Publishing)

Website:
https://www.facebook.com/thecompletecoach/

Available online at Amazon and Barnes and Noble:

https://www.amazon.com/

https://www.barnesandnoble.com

Dedication

"For all players who give coaches and give us the incredible privilege of helping you navigate along your tennis and life journey."
Tim Bainton and Jeremy Carl

A Special Thank You

Jeremy offers thanks to "Melissa, my wonderful and caring wife, and my beautiful daughter, Maggie - the most supportive wife and daughter a husband and father could ever ask for; to my parents and my brother who have always been there to encourage my passions and dreams; to the coaches who guided me as a player and competitor: David Redding, Jack Newman, Tim Siegel, Bobby McKee; and coaching mentors who always modeled for me what it means to be a good coach: Feisal Hassan and Mel Labat.

Jeremy dedicates this book to "my daughter, Maggie, who plays tennis and has put up with my coaching - good and bad - but still loves the sport. I hope that she continues to love tennis in a way that gives her inner joy and peace that lasts her a lifetime. I want her to know I will always be proud of what she does on and off the tennis court."

Tim offers thanks to "my parents for their selfless support of my tennis; my sister for always pushing me to be better; my Uncle John for his guidance and unconditional friendship; Paul Fisher for giving me the opportunity for coaching; Van Metre Companies for taking a risk and supporting my vision; and lastly, my beautiful and talented wife, Helen, who each day demands that I respect myself and show humility and kindness to the best of my abilities."

Table of Contents

Acknowledgments	11

Warming Up

Introduction	14
Jeremy's Journey	20
Tim's Tale	24
Why Tennis?	27
Jeremy's and Tim's Thoughts on Each Other	31

Point 1—Mental Mindset

Winning Is Never Easy	33
True Grit Metrics	38
Mental Myths	46
"Winning Only" Mindset vs. "Competitive" Mindset	49

Point 2—Healthy Environment

Playing for the Right Reasons	54
Parental Pressures	62
Healthy Parent/Child Tennis Relationship	
Lisa Goodman Stone	68
The Power of Low Positive Parenting	
Dr. William J. Carl III	76
What Parents and Kids Both Want from Tennis	
Linda Paul	82
Sibling's Take	
Sancha Legg	86
Coaching Expectations	90
High School, College or Pro—Where Will the Journey Take You?	97

What College Tennis Coaches Are Looking for In a Prospect
  David Redding 102
The Positive Role of Social Media in the Junior
  Journey—Digital Tattoos, the Footrace, and the Reflection
  Jenny Walls Robb 104
Nutrition for Junior Players: The Importance of Fueling-Up
  Dr. Charlotte Alabaster 107

Point 3—Elite Training for All Levels

Essential Qualities of Good Training 116
Power of Percentages—Singles and Doubles 121
Using Video Analysis Technology Wisely 133

Point 4—Athlete Based Foundation

Physical On-Court Competencies 137
Developing Agility, Speed, Balance, and Coordination for
  Tennis Players
  Dean Hollingworth 140
Good Techniques Equal Good Tactics 147
Move Smarter, Not Harder 155

Point 5—Match Day

Awareness Attributes of Champions—Singles and Doubles 160
Being a Problem Solver on the Court 168
Mastering the Tiebreak 171
Being Smarter Than the Cheater 173
Using Strategic Patterns for Doubles Success 175
Five Essential Qualities of Poaching 180
Top Ten Aspects of Doubles Communication 182

Point 6—Beyond the Court Life Skills

Transferable Life Skills –Part 1
   Sancha Legg   186
Transferable Life Skills – Part 2
   David Carl   189
Overcoming Adversity   194
Goal Setting   197

Point 7—Loving the Journey

Keys to Longevity   202
Keeping it Fun   205
Enjoying the Moment   208
WTA Player and Grand Slam Coach Offers Her Perspective
   Sarah Jane Stone   210
For the Love of the Game!
   Cristelle Grier Fox   222

Match Point

Final Thoughts   227
Glossary of Key Terms   228

Acknowledgments

We are eternally grateful to our family, friends and coaching colleagues who supported us and helped us turn this new book idea into a reality. First and foremost, we want to thank our parents for introducing us to the game of tennis in a way that allowed us to love the game and learn the life lessons it has taught us. Specifically, we want to thank Dr. William Carl III, well-known pastor, international public speaker and a published author of eight books himself, for editing our book and contributing to the book in a way that lays out for our readers a clear understanding of our coaching philosophy. We offer appreciation to Tim's wife, Helen, for doing the visual designs on the front and back cover. We also want to thank Sandy Davis for taking our picture again for this book and continuing to make us look better than we look in real life!

We also appreciate Lisa Stone, Dr. Charlotte Alabaster, Jenny Walls Robb, and Dean Hollingworth for their insightful and thoughtful contributions to the book. We also want to thank Sarah Jane Stone, former WTA pro player who coached Samantha Stosur, former grand slam champion, for her contributions. Also, former NCAA doubles champion Cristelle Grier Fox has written a beneficial chapter. We appreciate David Redding, head men's and women's tennis coach at Harding University, in Searcy, Arkansas, for writing a chapter on what college coaches looking for in junior players. It is wonderful to collaborate with such passionate and intelligent people as Lisa, Charlotte, Jenny, Dean, Sarah, David and Cristelle about the game.

We also appreciate Jeremy's Dad and Tim's Mom, Linda Paul, for a parent's perspective on a healthy family tennis environment. We are also grateful to Tim's sister, Sancha Legg, and Jeremy's brother, David Carl, for explaining how tennis skills and the game itself have been transferable in their professions. Even though they are not directly involved in tennis professionally, they never lost their love for the sport.

We also want to thank our fellow pros in the Alexandria, VA area— Daniele Albergottie, David Bryan, Michael Cable, Leon Cerdena, Brian Clay, Patrick Escalambre, Steve Fiske, Scott Hinkle, Dan Myers, Jona Roka, Mike Smith, Kelly Sykes and Jason Wnuk for their support through this process.

In addition, we appreciate Dimitris Kollaros, Gretchen Thompson, Kathleen O'Brien, and Celeste Jones both for supporting us in writing this book and in our professional development endeavors in general.

We are grateful to the USPTA for supporting our article ideas and the USTA Player Development Staff including Jessica Battaglia, Paul Lubbers and David Ramos for helping us grow as coaches through the USTA High Performance Program. We continue to appreciate the PTR and Peggy Edwards for supporting our ideas.

Tim thanks Andrew McPhee, Nestor Bernabe, Cameron Moore, Jim Harp, Brian Parkkonen, Erik Martinez, Bruce Hawtin, Bill Riddle, George Christoforatos, Jim Scott, Alice Hume, Frank Giampaolo and many more who have influenced his life and work.

Warming Up

Introduction

"Success is peace of mind which is a direct result of self-satisfaction in knowing you did your best to become the best you are capable of being."
John Wooden

Why another book written by a guy from Surrey, England and another guy from Dallas, Texas called *"The Complete Player?"* Here's why. We were talking about the experience of writing our first book, **The Complete Coach**, and how much we enjoyed it. So, we asked ourselves, "Why not write another book?" So, we did! What do we mean by the "The Complete Player?" It's a player who understands that environmental, technical, tactical, physical, and social components are equally important to a successful, enjoyable and lasting tennis journey.

The reality is this book could also be called the "The Complete Person." While we admit we are not experts on how to be perfect or complete by any stretch of the imagination, we do think this book provides excellent advice and insight on this important principle—being a complete player on the tennis court is exactly like being a complete person in life. You can't expect to be unprepared mentally, physically, socially or emotionally and succeed in tennis or life.

Today juniors have so many more distractions than we had as kids. Back then, after school, we had fewer options than children have today. Ours included mainly playing with friends, playing sports or doing homework. Now kids, as parents allow, can play a myriad of computer games, do social media or watch Netflix, to name a few. Jeremy remembers the internet not becoming fully utilized until he was in college. Yes, a world without the internet! Imagine that. How did society survive? So, with more distractions today, kids have more of a challenge staying focused on what represents a meaningful and productive use of time. Misuse of the internet is also a big problem for children and teenagers. For example, we, unfortunately, know of players who have lost college tennis scholarships because of inappropriate posts on social media.

We admit that it's impossible to cover every aspect of tennis in one book. Therefore we have divided our thoughts into these two books—**the coaching journey (first book) and the junior player journey (this book)**. In this book, we discuss navigating the junior tennis player journey. Because we decided to get some help dealing with as many aspects of the tennis journey as one can cover in one book, you will see contributions here by industry experts such as Lisa Goodman Stone, Jenny Walls Robb, and Dr. Charlotte Alabaster discussing essential issues such as healthy parent/child relationships, social media practices, and nutrition for tennis players, respectively. We are excited to have their involvement.

We are also excited to have other industry leaders and experts' involvement. We appreciate Dean Hollingworth's contribution on physical attributes of tennis training. Hollingsworth is a world-class expert, author, and speaker on fitness, conditioning, speed and agility training for tennis and other sports. We are also honored to have Sarah Stone, former WTA pro player, who competed in the main draw of Grand Slams, contributing to the book on her views, insights, and own personal reflections on navigating the junior tennis journey. Sarah is a world-class professional touring coach. Her former player and doubles partner, Samantha Stosur, won 3 grand slam titles during the time that she and Sarah worked together. In addition, Cristelle Grier Fox, an outstanding former NCAA player at Northwestern University and former tennis coach at Yale contributes insights that are invaluable to junior players of all ages coming up through the competitive ranks both here and abroad. We appreciate David Redding's insight on qualities college coaches are looking for in junior players. We are very grateful for all their insights.

From a family perspective, we appreciate Tim's sister and Jeremy's brother offering their takes on their tennis journeys. As we discussed in our first book, we think collaboration is an integral part of any person's professional and personal growth. We certainly don't know it all and would not be where we are without help along the way. This book includes passionate insights from world-class experts from the USA, the UK, Australia and Canada!

As we mentioned at the beginning of this introduction, we decided to use lessons we and others have learned to write about the "Complete Player" with an emphasis on the junior tennis player's journey. While we never won a Grand Slam ourselves, we did play high-level college tennis and have coached players who went on to play college tennis. More importantly, as experienced professional coaches to juniors of all levels, we have a genuine appreciation and love for the tennis journey. While this book is on the junior tennis player, there are many ideas and principles that an adult player can gain from reading this book as well. Even athletes in other sports can learn from the ideas presented in this book.

In our last book, **The Complete Coach**, we touched on the journey a coach takes to help make a positive impact on his/her students and the game during his/her career. Our goal for this book is to help all junior players, recreational to high-level competitive players, love and navigate the tennis journey for both singles and doubles. Our ideas come from our experiences working with all ranges of juniors from players just starting out to nationally ranked players as well as all types of club settings and environments—athletic clubs, outdoor swim and tennis clubs, country clubs, and high-end resorts. We view tennis as a sport to love for a lifetime, whatever your goals may be. This book is about loving the process. We hope you will see it is written with a genuine desire for all junior players to love their journey. It includes ideas, stories, philosophies, guidelines, and beliefs based on our journeys playing the game and continuing to learn about the game. This book is not about creating a guaranteed pathway to the pros, while that is a commendable goal to have.

You will see that the book is organized like our last book with seven main points identical to needing seven points to win a tie-break with each point being equally important. Specifically, we will discuss the following themes—**the mental side, a healthy environment, elite training for all levels, athletic based**

foundation, match day, beyond the court life skills, and loving the journey. You will notice many practical and accessible ideas, templates and philosophies presented here. Use the ones that help you the most. The book also includes stories from our tennis journeys related to the themes of various chapters. We like to think of this book as a blueprint for any junior level player looking to make a high school team or a college team, go pro or enjoy playing socially with your friends. In the book, we will examine the six components of player periodization—**physical, technical, tactical, strategic, mental and environmental,** not in a list form but a comprehensible and authentic way that will be helpful to you.

Also, this is more than a book of the best tips for forehands, backhands, volleys, overheads, serve or return of serve. While good tips on basic strokes are essential and will be discussed during parts of the book, our goal as authors is to help you be the best possible player on the court and best person off the court in life. Plus, we feel there is already great advice out there on strokes, and we hope you can combine our thoughts with those existing tips to help you meet your tennis goals. Also, as proponents of the 10U progression teaching philosophy using the ROGY (red, orange, green, yellow) ball progression, we certainly see the value in that and would ask that any suggestions in this book are applied with appropriate age equipment and court size. The book will touch on the five basic phases of play - **serving, returning, baseline play, you coming to net and your opponent coming to the net.** Finally, any technical tips for hitting certain shots will apply for singles and doubles.

Now a warning. If you are not interested in either excellence or success, then stop reading now because this book is about both. However, if you do want to excel and succeed in life through tennis, then keep reading. In addition, the book focuses on the "process of excellence and success" not just winning. Before we begin, we want to share a brief word about success, which forms the foundation for all our thoughts presented in this book.

What defines success for a player? Is it being ranked in your age group? Is it making your high school team or a college team? There is no definite answer; it could be one, any, or none of these. That's the thing about success—it is only measured subjectively for each player. We believe John Wooden's quote at the very beginning of the introduction sums it up well. Differences in the meaning of success are created by differences in player's goals. Whatever your goal, make sure it's realistic, or you will find yourself setting the bar too high, thus setting yourself up for failure. This is a concept we will discuss in more detail in later chapters.

So how do you go about measuring success? It's very likely you don't even know what success means for you, and that's perfectly fine. Let's make one thing very clear. It does not mean being perfect, especially in tennis. It also does not mean assuming that anything is guaranteed in tennis. The only thing that is guaranteed in a match is you will win, or you will lose, and you can't control that outcome. There will be players as good as you, better than you and worse than you, just like in life.

Many successful tennis players had speed bumps along the way, but they only viewed them as speed bumps, not roadblocks. For example, Sloane Stephens, right after winning the 2017 US Open, recounted the story of a coach once telling her she would only ever play Division II college tennis. Or Novak Djokovic having to learn some of his tennis in an empty swimming pool due to living in a war-torn country as a kid. Or Stan Smith being rejected as a ball boy for lack of coordination but ended up being a Grand Slam champion later. Finally, Andre Agassi being No. 1 in the world and then falling outside the top 100, but then by refocusing on his game and training to return to No. 1 in the world. We like to say all these players had this philosophy about their tennis journey—**love it, learn it and live it**, which we will discuss later in the book. Even though Agassi admits that he initially hated tennis, he grew to love it. So, know that not everyone's journey is the same, nor should it be. Remember that the tennis journey has peaks and valleys, and success comes from treating the valleys as learning experiences, not failures. Their true passion for the game helped put their valley experiences in the right perspective relative to their overall tennis journeys. We both had speed bumps throughout our journey, but we both ended up being able to play college tennis on scholarship.

Realizing what kind of person, you are is the best way to understand how to define success for yourself in tennis. Are you a person who needs to see results? Would you be content with moving up to number one on your high school team and not playing college tennis or the pros? Asking self-directed questions such as these and trusting the right people along the journey provides the first step toward defining success.

In our last book, we talked about the best advice that we can give for realizing success is to "start small, dream big." While this can apply to junior players, we will touch on how to handle expectations and dreams that junior players may have. Success cannot always be defined by the end goal. Through time and effort, you will come to make your mark in tennis and the world, even if the original goal doesn't work out. In short, the definition of success varies from player to player. To become successful, players need to know what success means for them, and what their vision for the future is. One message we hope readers take from this book is this—**goals in life can be achieved, but it takes the right philosophy, vision, mentors, and passion to help you achieve them.** We admit that as kids we never said, "we're going to write a book one day," but the ideas just mentioned led us to this point in our lives. We are grateful for those people who encouraged and believed in us. In other words, never say never!

In this book, we explore different avenues to success for you as a player. Now, we hope you will learn from what we have learned in a way that will help you enjoy your tennis journey more than you ever have before!

Jeremy's Journey

It was September 11, 2001. It seemed like a typical day in Washington, D.C., and yet we know there was nothing ordinary about it. As long as I live I will never forget that day just as my parents will always remember the day JFK was shot and my grandparents will never forget the day Pearl Harbor was attacked. I was a young Capitol Hill staffer working for U.S. Senator Kay Bailey Hutchison of Texas, my home state at the time. I had graduated from Presbyterian College in Clinton, S.C. in 2000 and was getting my professional work life started in Washington, D.C. I was staying in my college roommate's apartment, sleeping on an air mattress. He had moved to DC a year earlier. I lived in the Alexandria, VA area near Old Town Alexandria about a 30-minute drive on a good traffic day into the Hart Senate Office Building on Capitol Hill.

    That morning, I got a late start and had no idea I would pass right by the Pentagon not long before a plane crashed into it. I remember having the radio on and hearing something about a plane hitting a building in New York City. I thought how awful that was but did not understand how world-changing an event it was until I got to work. When I arrived, I noticed everyone glued to the TVs in the Senate office with the News blaring the story as a commercial plane flew right into one of the World Trade Centers. Then a couple of minutes later the same thing happened to other World Trade Center, then the Pentagon with the Shanksville, PA crash to follow, the plane that had been headed for the Capitol Building. The Hill was given the evacuate order. So, Senator Hutchison quickly and calmly gathered all the staff and let us know we had two choices—we could either try to get home with certain roads blocked off or go to her house on Capitol Hill. Since I knew I'd never make it past the Pentagon which had just been hit, I decided to go with the Senator and other staff who made the same decision. As soon as we arrived at her house, we watched in complete horror as the two World Trade Centers collapsed.

I will never forget this next part for the rest of my life. Once in the Senator's house, she immediately got on her computer for all of us to email our loved ones about our safety because all the cell phone connections were blocked. My dad remembers his and my mom's panic trying unsuccessfully to reach me. The Senator sat right next to me, not as my boss, but as a shepherd protecting her flock. She made sure that I typed in my parents' email address and sent the message "I am okay" to them and did the same with the rest of the staff. My parents lived in Texas at the time. Out of all the things she did as Senator, I know the care she showed for me and her staffers' safety that day was the single greatest and most appreciated action she ever did as a Senator. In a way this message can be translated into coaching because coaching is not about teaching the perfect forehand stroke but about guiding players in purposeful problem solving so they know (while nothing can compare to the horror of 9/11) everything "will be okay" even during the most stressful times of their matches.

Even though working in politics both for a United States Senator and the President of United States at the White House provided incredible experiences, I decided in the summer of 2008 to take the plunge full time in the tennis teaching world. While working in 2007 as Associate Director of External Affairs in the Public and Congressional Affairs Office of the National Credit Union Administration in Alexandria, VA, I began volunteering on weekends coaching some tennis classes at Regency Sport and Health in McLean, VA. I knew pretty quickly that tennis coaching was something I always felt I might be called to pursue. I emailed USPTA Master Professional Feisal Hassan, Tennis Director of Regency Sport and Health in McLean, VA at the time. He gave me a call, and we spoke about my interest in exploring tennis teaching as a profession, and just getting a feel for it. After I had volunteered initially by assisting with classes, he let me know of a full-time opening that could start in the summer of 2008. I decided to take it and leave government service for good. My initial experience working for Feisal was an incredible introduction to the essential principles of coaching.

But let me go back to the beginning. Tennis has been my lifelong passion, introduced and inspired by my parents. I was born August 19, 1977, in Richmond, Virginia. My first experience with tennis was when I was 18 months old, and my parents hung a Nerf ball on a string in an archway of our house. I would whack away at that ball with a racquetball racquet for hours at a time.

In retrospect I realize my parents never pushed me into tennis; instead, they merely presented the game to me and let me enjoy it. I remember going to Wimbledon when I was 11 years old. One day we were at Centre Court watching Boris Becker who was about to become the 1989 Wimbledon Champion. I turned to my dad and said, "I am going to come back here someday." He said, "Okay." I said, "I mean to play." He said, "That sounds great!" The important thing was the fact that he let me figure out on my own how to strive to compete at a very high level. Now, every day as I play with my daughter Maggie, I apply those same principles.

It is no surprise that my parents would have me involved in tennis since they both enjoyed the sport from their high school years on. My mom played on her high school tennis team, and my dad played it recreationally in high school. When they met at the University of Tulsa, Dad noticed immediately how well Mom played and decided to focus on improving his own game as quickly as he could to impress Mom. Now at almost 70 he still plays competitively.

My parents also instilled a love for the game in my brother, David, who is an accomplished actor on stage, television, and film and a stand-up comedian in New York City. While he never pursued a career in tennis, he has always had a passion for the game. Anytime we see each other we still enjoy playing tennis. When we moved to Texas, I was five years old. In junior high and high school, I played regularly in USTA Championship level tournaments throughout the state. I played college tennis at Presbyterian College in Clinton, S.C. and was captain of the team my senior year helping lead my fellow players to victory as South Atlantic Conference Champions.

As mentioned earlier, once I graduated from college in 2000, I moved to Washington, D.C. to get experience working in a government job. After serving on the Legislative Staff on Senator Hutchison and subsequently in the White House, I decided to return to my real passion—Tennis. Following a successful career of coaching in the DC Metropolitan area, I joined my coauthor, Tim Bainton, at Mount Vernon Athletic Club as part of the Blue Chip Academy teaching regionally and nationally ranked high-end juniors. Tim and I have been fortunate to learn from each other and help grow the game through our common coaching experiences. Now I teach at Belle Haven Country Club in Alexandria, VA.

My family has always been passionate about education and teaching. My mom, a math and political science major at the University of Tulsa, grew up with a love for education since her mother was a school teacher in Maryville, TN and her dad a school principal. My dad has served as Senior Pastor at First Presbyterian Church in Dallas, TX, President and Professor at Pittsburgh Theological Seminary and currently serves as Senior Pastor of Independent Presbyterian Church in Birmingham, AL. Dad always says a good sermon, "must teach the mind, touch the heart and move the will." A good tennis lesson does the same—teach a skill, inspire joy and move the player to turn focused practice into skilled match play.

Finally, I have a very supportive wife named Melissa who, though not a tennis player herself, continues to be supportive of my decision to change from government work to teaching tennis full time. She has been a big encourager in all the coaching endeavors I have pursued. Her parents also have a background in education since her mom is a former school principal and her dad a high school biology teacher and counselor.

Tim's Tale

The year was 1994 and stars filled the night sky as I watched my hero Stefan Edberg play live for the very first time. The match was held over for bad light but for an eleven-year-old who had fallen in love with tennis, it was magic. I can visualize it like it was yesterday - the beauty of Centre Court, the quiet followed by the roars of the crowd and the beauty of Edberg's game. Another profound moment in my tennis life was in 1999, the final day of the USA vs. GBR Davis Cup tie in Birmingham, England. I attended the event with a group of fellow Surrey teammates organized by my coach. Although we were mildly upset that Great Britain lost the tie, I can still remember the excitement and happiness that filled the air. I can also remember going across the street to a neighbor's house, the only place with cable, to watch the French Open final with my dad the year Muster won.

I was born January 6th, 1983 in Carshalton, and spent all my life in the traditional English village of Chobham Surrey. As a 10-year-old, I was told I wasn't allowed to play on the Village Men's tennis team because "I kept beating all of the players." I later played at Queens Club where I would attend practices and leave school early to attend tournaments.

Playing County Cup for the formidable Surrey with many ATP players as teammates, becoming the 16 and under state champion as a 14-year-old, playing nationals, ITF, internationally: tennis was my identity and I became a part of my generation's rising junior tennis star fabric in the United Kingdom.

I played all sports and loved every minute of it, but it was a profound summer back in 1993 that changed my life forever. I attended a tennis camp at the Chris Lane Tennis Club in Woking, Surrey, and there I met the first coach who would forever shape my love and appreciation for tennis and the art of coaching. Her name was Claire Pollard. I have never been so excited to wake up and do anything in my life because of Claire, a truly magnetizing coach that has gone on to do great things.

Next, I worked with the up and coming legend Justin Sherring, a guy who taught me how to be determined, disciplined and selfless. He would work with me three mornings a week at 6:30 AM for free and then take me to school. He believed in me and looking back I will never be able to express my lifelong appreciation for what he did. Justin was getting into teaching and determined to be a coach for the same reasons I became one: because he wanted to! He had a larger-than-life personality despite being 5'6 on a good day. However, he would take me to tournaments, support me, root for me and be there for me. He has gone on to make his mark in the game of tennis, and I appreciate all he did for me.

My tennis abilities took me to every part of the country and beyond, competing every weekend on the Adidas Junior circuit that was for the top 16 players in the country. It was quite an experience to leave school on a Friday, do my homework on a train to random places such as Darlington, Sunderland, and Wrexham to arrive at midnight to some affordable hotel, play four matches in two days, return and then attend school again Monday morning. These times were the best of times.

I attended St. George's College in Weybridge on a tennis scholarship, and my game truly thrived there. The school had so many assets for tennis players to utilize, and all types of courts: clay, grass, and hard as well as both indoor and outdoor courts. The school was a hotbed for young talent and a warm-up venue for Wimbledon where I had seen many top players develop. I established a strong bond with the faculty at the school. I dearly loved Mr. Peak, the headmaster, and a man of incredible integrity, Mr. Witter, an American with more wit than you could imagine who taught English, Ms. Frawley, an Oxbridge-educated tutor who taught me the value of attendance, discipline, and respect. Mr. Watters, a genius of a teacher who taught my 'A' level politics and philosophy classes, taught me how to think, to be challenged and to improve continuously in everything I did. I truly loved those days, and through exceptional teaching, without knowing it, they provided me a backbone for great coaching.

Now to answer the "Why did you come to America?" question. I arrived in Fairfax VA, to attend the mighty George Mason University seven days before 9/11. In reflection, being in a foreign land with such a tragedy occurring on your doorstep meant that my illusions of playing one year of college tennis on a gap year and then returning to a deferred place at the London School of Economics were forever gone. This was my home and my family for four years and beyond. The Northern Virginia, DC area has been home and a place to build a business, family, friends, and opportunity ever since.

After school, I went into coaching despite opportunities to move into many other professions; this is where I wanted to be. I started from scratch earning $9 an hour in 2005 to becoming one of the most successful industry leaders in the country a decade later. The key is to be always learning, treat everyone equally and bring as many people into your world as possible. Stay hungry, stay humble and ultimately never stop loving the art of coaching.

Why Tennis?

Why Tennis? Simple. Whatever profession you choose in life tennis can help you in some positive way. If you take anything away from this book, please understand this point. This is not hot air for you to keep reading our book. It is the truth. Let's look at some data on this that speaks to the correlation between men and women playing tennis as juniors and being successful leaders.

An article from **Fortune** titled *What do 65% of the Most Powerful Women Have in Common?* suggests the answer is Sports, (online, Valentina Zarya, September 22, 2017) mentioning that "The women on the 2017 *Fortune* list of Most Powerful Women (MPW) are no exception. Of the 31 MPWs who responded to *Fortune*'s query, 20 (65%) played sports competitively in either high school or college; sometimes both. The most popular sport was a three-way tie between swimming, basketball, and **tennis**." The current head of the USTA (United States Tennis Association), Katrina Adams, played on the pro tennis circuit herself. She started playing tennis at six years of age. She also played high school tennis and at Northwestern University, where she was twice voted All-American. Tennis has undoubtedly been a part of women leaders' lives early on as shown from previously mentioned statistics.

Some impressive facts also can be highlighted when it comes to male CEO's. In an article from **Business Insider**, titled *The Five Biggest Jock CEOs* (online, Tony Manfred, July 7, 2011), two of the five CEOS mentioned played tennis. Former Ford CEO Alan Mulally played on a semi-professional tennis circuit and **Time Magazine** called him an "avid" tennis player in 2008. Former Micron Technology CEO, Steven Appleton, played pro tennis in the 1980s. He earned a tennis scholarship to Boise State, and after graduating in 1982, he spent six months playing pro tennis on the satellite circuit.

Let's get back to us. Fortunately, we were introduced to tennis in a manner by our parents that planted the seed for our love for the game. As former top juniors and now as coaches who have experienced all levels of the game, tennis has taught us to be better persons, coaches, businessmen, friends and life strategists. We know the term "life strategist" seems a bit ridiculous, but as this book will show you, tennis is a sport that has so many transferable skills from the court to the reality of life. Because throughout our lives we have learned from tennis constantly, we have been able to navigate life more effectively. We realize that's quite a statement!

So, we hope this book will help you determine the importance of tennis in how it impacts everything you do in your life. We have decided to take the skill of playing and training for tennis and relate it to the real world in which you the reader live and relate how the skills you have learned in tennis can help you navigate issues and circumstances beyond the court.

Listen to this story about one of our players and how tennis became a positive influence on him. It was a hot, humid, 100-degree summer day in Washington, D.C. when one of our players won the 2015 Citi Open Future Stars of Tomorrow tournament at Fitzgerald Tennis Center in Washington, D.C. It coincided with the Citi Open ATP/WTA Tournament in Washington, D.C in the historic Rock Creek Park. His parents were very excited for their son's achievement as he played top-ranked tournament players from other clubs and programs in the Mid-Atlantic area. Our player during the trophy presentation was on cloud nine having played numerous close matches against very tough competitors. What happened next was one of the most incredible acts of sportsmanship we have ever seen as coaches. During the ceremony, as players were receiving their trophies, the runner-up dropped his on the ground. Our player who won first place, immediately seeing the disappointment and embarrassment on the face of his competitor because he had dropped his trophy, gave his trophy to his competitor. The sheer joy on the face of the runner-up and the obvious relief seen on his parents' faces in response to our player's selfless act was one of the most rewarding things we have ever witnessed beyond seeing one of our students win a tournament.

We believe that tennis provides these moments of truth in life that can teach such values as sportsmanship and respect for others. While we will never know if we had a direct influence on our player's decision to give away his trophy, we know that tennis being healthily introduced to him must have played a positive role in what he did that day. Tennis certainly has helped us be better people even though we know we are not perfect by a longshot, which our family and closest friends will confirm!

In life, we think of people in two categories – complainers or conquerors. The complainer's attitude in life means he/she meets every challenge with a "woe is me" outlook. A complainer spends more time complaining about problems in contrast to finding solutions. On the other hand, a conqueror's attitude in life means he/she understands that success comes from putting your head down and looking to solve the problem, which can include being willing to collaborate with like-minded problem solvers on a topic. We are not perfect in being conquerors, but we certainly strive to be. In tennis, we have observed that the most successful players have the conqueror's attitude. This outlook applies to any level of play—recreational, high-level tournament or pro players. In our immediate profession of coaching, we are daily problem solvers.

However, we have learned by working in other fields professionally that no one likes a complainer. This is true in marriages, friendships and other areas of life. Tennis matches teach players three primary values: **resiliency,** meaning a tennis player can always come back until the match is over, **accountability for decisions** made and the **ability to handle adversity** healthily. These are all life skills and attributes **happy and successful** people have. We also hope this book helps guide junior players in principles that lead to positive, productive, and purposeful lives. As we noted earlier, young people have many more influences pulling them in different directions today than we had when we were growing up.

In our first book, we talk about the great advice that Wayne Bryan, father and coach for the Bryan Brothers, the most successful doubles team ever on the pro circuit, said to participants in a clinic we were helping him coach at the ATP/WTA Citi Open in Washington, D.C. in the summer of 2017. He said, "We (he and his wife) always guided our boys to what made them happy and knew success would follow." For parents of tennis players, we hope you think about that statement as you read this book. Be careful about thinking you can guarantee "success" for your child in tennis. Start with happiness first. Trust us. You will be glad you did. Now let's get started talking about the most wonderful journey anyone could ever take. However, before we do that we each want to make a quick statement about each other.

Jeremy's and Tim's Thoughts on Each Other

We certainly are grateful to collaborate on our second book in a way that we hope will allow you to see our respect for each other and our desire to make the industry and the game better for coaches, parents, and players through the wisdom and experience shared in this book.

Jeremy on his co-author

As a friend and colleague, Tim is the embodiment of respect, support, and encouragement. I am grateful for his unselfish desire to help me grow professionally in all aspects of my coaching. His drive to pass along his knowledge to others and learn from others makes it a pleasure to work with him and call him a partner. His passion to improve people's lives on and off the court through tennis is always evident in his daily actions. His commitment and hunger for excellence in the tennis industry and as a person has made him a leader in tennis, coaching, business and mentoring.

Tim on his co-author

Jeremy is one of the most gracious, loyal and intelligent friends and colleagues that I know. He defines the professional coach: always on time, always presentable, and always prepared. He is a coach who lives his life by the same standard that he demands of his students. His passion and love for the game and the art of coaching have solidified him as one of the best development coaches in the country and a respected force on improving the industry through continuing education, writing and speaking.

Point 1
Mental Mindset

Winning Is Never Easy

"It's not whether you get knocked down,
it's whether you get up."
Vince Lombardi

"If we all trained our minds as much as we are training our muscles and physical body, I think we would achieve and maximize our potential. We don't know how much we can really achieve until we have this kind of mindset of wanting always to evolve and improve. I believe in the power of the mind and visualization, which is a big part of my everyday life."
Novak Djokovic

Before we get into the specifics of this chapter, let's talk about why our first point is about the mental side of tennis. It's very simple. The foundation for being a great player or coach starts with solid mental acumen. It's where the tennis journey begins, so our book begins here too.

Let's look at some data to illustrate why the mindset is so important. An article in **The Wall Street Journal**, titled "How Much Tennis is played during a Match?" (Stu Woo, Online, September 4, 2013), examined the amount of time tennis players "actually played" during a match. In two matches that were studied, only 17.5% of the time was spent playing, which means 82.5% of the time was not. In the article, which covers both singles and doubles play, the author noted that "One of the matches we scrutinized was a second-round, four-setter between Leonardo Mayer and defending champion Andy Murray. The entire match lasted two hours and 41 minutes—three minutes shorter than the average men's singles match at last year's U.S. Open. Mayer and Murray actively played for 26 minutes and 29 seconds, or only 16.4% of the time.

"We also broke out the stopwatch for another match, a one-hour-and-26-minute women's doubles tilt between Daniela Hantuchova and Martina Hingis and the world's top-ranked team of Sara Errani and Roberta Vinci. We figured there would be more down time in doubles since teammates discuss strategy before every point. However, compared with the men's singles match, this one featured plenty of action, with 16 minutes and 50 seconds of tennis, or 19.6% of the match time. The women served fewer aces and hit fewer service winners, resulting in more prolonged points."

It's clear that the author of this article has hit on an important statistic that highlights one of the crucial elements of any sport, especially tennis. The quotations by Djokovic and legendary football coach Vince Lombardi at the beginning of this chapter demonstrate their understanding of the importance of the mental side of sports.

With the mental aspect of tennis in mind, let's look at its impact on the ability to win a tennis match. The reality is winning will never be easy in tennis. You might be saying what if I win 6-0, 6-0? Yes, the score might indicate that it was easy. However, each game could have gone to deuce, or it could have been a hot or windy day. Let's say each game was a blowout to you. We would argue it is still not easy. Why? In tennis, the result of a point in a match is decided by the independent decision-making of each player. Here's another example. Let's say one player gets hurt during the match with a leg cramp or something else but can still finish playing to the end. This should be a cakewalk for the non-injured player, right? Again, the answer is no. This happens at every level. We have had this happen to us, and you see it with pros also. Let's not forget Michael Chang who won his French Open title with massive leg cramps to finish the match against Ivan Lendl. Lendl should have won? Right? Yes, you'd think so. We can't go back in time and get in the heads of the players, but we can make a general comment on the state of this situation. When one player is injured, the pressure is now entirely on the non-injured player because the injured player has nothing to lose. The non-injured player can start thinking, "I hope I don't become a choke artist!" The basic strategy for the non-inured player should be to forget that the other player is injured and keeping your focus on playing the best you can. The injured player knows his/her body and knows when to stop. A good mental mindset is crucial for the non-injured player in situations like this. In the same way, the ability of a player to win a point down match point with a winning passing shot on the dead run has much more to with that player's mental mindset than with technical skill. While their technical ability helps a player hit the needle-threading shot, the basis for getting to the shot comes primarily from that player's mental mindset as well as his/her determination never to give up.

For a player to be successful in a match, they need to focus on the following components of their game in this order – **mindset, footwork, and technical and tactical execution**. We have seen many players get into trouble in matches, and instead of returning to a correct mindset, they start thinking about how technically incorrect their shots are. If players would learn to reset to a more positive right attitude, they would be able to recalibrate their game and eventually win the match. We like to call this the **competitive focus chain**. Players need to get the mind ready to move the feet, and the feet ready to move to the ball to apply the right technical skill. Once players can do that, they can employ the tactics they want to win.

And now a warning for any parents reading this chapter. You can have a massive influence on your child's mental state (read more about this crucial point in the chapters in Point 2 **Healthy Environment**). Never tell your kids before a tournament "you should win this match." It does not matter if your child is the top seed and your child has beaten the player he/she is about to play every other time, or you know the player he/she is about to play is new to playing in this level of the tournament. We know this partly because we have made this exact mistake as coaches in our prepping our players for upcoming matches. We would be lying if we said we never did this ourselves. By saying "you should win this match," you are putting unneeded pressure on your child. The reality is this is not your role as a parent. As the parent, you should be an encourager, never heightening expectations. Unneeded pressure should never be put on a player before a match. Unfortunately, the sheer need for parents to see their children "win" gets in the way of players learning to "enjoy the experience." The only thing that should be applied before a match is positive inspiration for players to play their very best. There are not many absolutes in tennis, but we feel from our experiences as coaches, and Jeremy as a parent of a player himself, this is critical. In other words, saying "you should win this match" to your child makes the idea that winning a match should be easy when in reality winning any match is never easy. Also, the only message for your child that will result from losing this match, even if it's close and a great match, is your child failed. And that is never a prescription for "loving the journey." It's a message that only shortens the tennis journey and leads to early burnout when you as a parent hope tennis will be a sport that will last a lifetime for your child. For all coaches, this admonishment applies to us as well. We like to call this the "look ahead" sin of tennis parenting or coaching. It may sound harsh for us to put it this way, but we think it's very relevant and important. A phrase that might work better before a match is "play your best and give it all you've got." The truth of the matter is if your child is the better player he/she will probably win.

Jeremy's daughter recently was in a play that her after-school program produced. Jeremy remembers the director of the play reminding all the parents that every part in the play will be crucial and important. She told a quick story of overhearing a parent one time say to their child, "You must get the top role." Wow! Talk about setting up your child to feel like a failure. The director correctly made the point that this was not what she wanted us to do as parents. Jeremy has no idea what happened with that child, but he was glad that the person in charge of directing his child in the play had the right approach toward guiding and inspiring kids. Like any good and worthwhile experience in life tennis matches, as this example aptly demonstrates, should be based on inspiring kids.

Summary

In tennis, especially singles, once the match starts you are on an island by yourself being watched by others but accountable for your actions. It is a lonely sport but one that can be incredibly empowering and inspiring at the same time with the right mindset. In the next several chapters we will touch on other specific aspects of the mental mindset.

True Grit Metrics

"Concentration and mental toughness are
the margins of victory."
Bill Russell

As we discussed in the previous chapter, research has shown more of the time in a match is spent not hitting the ball versus hitting the ball or moving during the point. The importance of this concept is certainly explained well in such books as **The Inner Game of Tennis** by Timothy Gallwey, **The Mental Game by** James E. Loehr, **Intelligent Tennis** by Skip Singleton, **Think to Win** by Allen Fox, **Winning Ugly** by Brad Gilbert, and more humorously **Tennis by Machiavelli** by Simon Ramo. In our first book, **The Complete Coach**, we discussed the use of "Mental Metrics" to evaluate players' mental side of tennis during a match. In this chapter, we will discuss more specifically the characteristic of mental toughness in a player during the challenging parts of the match. Jeremy, Tim, and Dr. William J. Carl III -- who has a Ph.D. in Communications and was the contributor and driving force behind the thoughts for the "Mental Metrics" chapter in our first book -- all contributed to this chapter.

    In this chapter we would like to introduce the idea of a "true grit mindset," a mindset that applies to everyone whether you are playing at the pro, college, junior or adult league or club level. The "true grit mindset" is what carries you through during the non-playing times in a match, and often makes the difference between winning and losing. Having a "true grit mindset" helps players avoid the deadly "mental meltdown." Every great athlete has true grit qualities. We are not talking here about the John Wayne classic western "True Grit" released in 1969 even though that was a great movie. We mean qualities players show when they could be giving up due to tough circumstances, but still fight on and either end up victorious or just knowing they gave it their all.

Moments we are referring to include Pete Sampras' win in the 1996 US Open match against Alex Corretja, a grueling five-set match in which Sampras vomited twice, but still won the match. Or Michael Chang serving underhand to Ivan Lendl in the 1989 French Open Final because of his massive leg cramps and still managed to win. While these are amazing comeback moments in our sport, "True Grit" is also the way players are telegraphing their body language. For instance, Jimmy Connors at the age of 39 made his run to US Open semifinals with powerful, confident body language all the way to the end. In this chapter, we will discuss key body language attributes we have noticed that are vital to helping players succeed in the tight, tough moments of a match.

Check out these statements from Stefan Edberg and Ivan Lendl which speak to a "true grit mindset." Edberg referring to his two set from behind comeback win at the 1988 Wimbledon semifinals against Miloslav Mecir said this: "I wouldn't have won today if I didn't have guts." Lendl, referring to his 1984 French Open win over John McEnroe after being down two sets to love and playing against McEnroe who had a 39-match winning streak before the match, said that "I felt that once I could break, I could do it again."

Nadal once said this about body language during a grand slam final, "No, I was not calm. I was nervous, but all the body language that is not in a positive way is stupid to make because it's going against you. [It] is one of the things that I tried to do all my life, that the body language helps me, not go against me. Because [body language] is one of the things that depends **just on me, not on the opponent**."

We have also had our moments of true grit in our playing. Jeremy recalls as a 13-year-old playing in a tournament at Kiest Park in Dallas, Texas to have a chance to move up to the Championship division in the USTA Texas section. The tournament was called at the time a ZAT, which stood for Zonal Area Tournament (now called Challenger Tournament). In one of his matches toward the end of the tournament, he got down 6-0, 5-0 and remembers that he was never going to give up. Well, to everyone's surprise, especially his opponent, Jeremy ended up coming back on that hot summer day to win the match and move through the rest of the tournament draw enough to qualify for the Championship level division. He remembers his determination to stay positive during that match was a springboard moment of truth for him continuing his junior tennis journey. At some point in your journey, you will have *true grit* moments which we hope you can look back on and be proud of years later.

What can we take away from these stories and quotes? It's this: your body language and mindset are controlled by you regardless of the circumstances. You can't control such things as the score, the wind, the surface, or the style of play your opponent brings to the match. Nadal's statement and his performance year in and year out tells the story. He recognizes that his body language responses come down to choices he makes regardless of what his opponent is doing.

We like to use the following "True Grit Metrics" as a way for you as a player to determine how well you are doing with the non-match playing elements of your game: **posture, eyes, facial expression, hands, feet, keeping routines, deep breaths, positive reactions, calmness during changeovers, and confident strides.** Here they are in more detail.

Posture—Positive body language for posture is evident when a player's shoulders are relaxed with one's back straight, but not rigid. By contrast, negative body language would appear when the player's shoulders are slumped.

Eyes—During stressful times in a match it is very easy to look at other courts, look in the stands for parents' or coaches' support, or do other things that take away from focusing on the match. Great champions know how to keep their eye on the prize and stay in the moment. They are aware of what they can control. They do things like after each point keep their eyes focused on straightening strings, looking at the ball when bouncing it a certain number of times before serving, or going from looking at their strings to looking at the opponent next when returning serve. Their eyes stay fixed on the items that matter during each moment of play.

Facial Expression—During tough times great players keep smiling or show determination in their faces and never frown. They display an attitude of being "unbroken." They might feel stress inside but never show it.

Hands—Players hands are relaxed. They don't look like they are afraid someone is going to run on the court and try to snatch the racquet out of his or her hand. When walking between points, their hands are not clenching their racquet. For example, players may put their racquet in their non-dominant hand and straighten their strings as a way of relaxing. Players also have relaxed hands when receiving serves or about to serve themselves.

Feet—Players keep on the balls of their feet between points, especially when returning serves. They walk from return position to return position with a spring in their step. Tennis is a game of footwork first. Think about how Nadal, regardless of the score, gets up with a spring in his step when going back on the court after every single changeover.

Keep Routines—All players have routines such as how many times they bounce the ball before a serve, spinning the racquet a certain amount of times before receiving serve, or certain rituals during a changeover. Federer and Agassi are players who spin their racquets before returning their serves. We remember reading one article where it said Nadal has 19 different routines. If you watch Nadal closely before every serve, you will see several of these little rituals, routine twitches. If players are still calm during stressful times, they tend to keep their routines.

Deep Breaths—One of the most prominent body language techniques we have learned in our continuing education programs is how well players control their breathing. We realize this sounds simple, but it is essential, especially during pressure times of a match. The mental side of tennis involves knowing how to control the body as well as the mind. We have learned from both our junior playing days and from coaching that deep breaths help relax the mind, therefore helping overcome negative thoughts. Let's look at some research on this topic. In an article by Lesley Alderman, "Breathe. Exhale. Repeat: The Benefits of Controlled Breathing," from *The New York Times*, November 9, 2016, the author points out that controlled breathing has been shown to reduce stress and increase alertness. This same article mentions that "changing the way you breathe appears to send a signal to the brain to adjust the parasympathetic branch of the nervous system, which can promote a feeling of calm."

Positive Reactions—Positive reactions come with fist pumps when hitting a great shot or positive self-talk when winning a point. On the other hand, when missing a shot, it helps to take a deep breath then close your eyes and visualize hitting the shot you want to hit.

Calmness during Changeovers—This means remaining calm and not agitated while sitting down between games. It also means drinking water and toweling off in the same way as always or looking at notes you've written down about the match. You can see Andy Murray and other top players looking at notes about their game plans during changeovers. **A good test of this is if you are in the audience and you don't** know the score of the match, you would not know if a player is ahead or behind by watching that player during a changeover. Throwing or breaking a racquet during a changeover is a real no-no if you want to win.

Confident Strides—All your movements between points should have both purpose and confidence. Even if you are behind, you never show it. In fact, you may appear that you are winning to someone who doesn't know the score.

As previously mentioned early in this chapter, in our first book, **The Complete Coach**, we discussed a way of measuring the mental aspects of a player during a match called "Mental Metrics." We can use a similar system for "True Grit Metrics." As a player, you can use this *10 to 1* scale (10 being the highest) to rate each area of your play after your match. This can be done by your coach also. Add up each area of scores from a match when you are down two games or more and one game away from losing a set, and you will have your grade out of 100. For example, if a player is down

5-3 (or more) in a set, if you had a score of 70 or above, it means you gave yourself a good chance through body language to come back and win! This can be done when you are ahead in the same fashion, and in that case, would be called "Close Out Metrics."

Below is an example of this system from a match Jeremy's daughter, Maggie, played during a 10 and under Girls tournament at College Park, MD on 2/25/2018. She was down 3-1 then came back and almost won the match. The match was a short set, first to 4 games.

Match: 10 and Under Girls Orange Level 1
Date: 2/25/2018
Score When Started Charting: Down 3-1
Match Format: First to Four Games
Result: Lost 4-3

	Grade	Comments
Posture	10	Back was straight but not rigid, with shoulders relaxed
Eyes	7	Your eyes were mostly fixed on your strings between points or on your opponent as she was bouncing the ball to serve, but sometimes you were looking at other courts instead of your match
Facial Expression	9	You were smiling when you hit a good shot or staying determined even when your opponent hit a good shot
Hands	6	Your hands could have been more relaxed when holding your racquet between points

Feet	10	You were always walking around with a spring in your step and were on the balls of your feet before returning every serve
Keeping Routines	9	You were keeping your routines before serving
Deep Breaths	10	You were taking controlling slow breaths during points
Positive Reactions	9	You were showing positive reactions to the good shots you hit
Calmness during Changeover	9	You kept composed during every changeover
Confident Strides	8	Your strides between points were confident and purposeful
Total Score	87	

As you can see from this example with Jeremy's daughter that having "True Grit Metrics" does not necessarily mean that you will win the match, but it does mean you will keep in perspective the vital non-match, mental aspects of playing to win.

Sometimes it can be as simple as looking back on something positive you did in a previous match. Jeremy remembers when he was coaching the 16 and under Boys and Girls Zonals L2 USTA Mid-Atlantic team. One of his players was having a very tough match down 6-0, 5-0. His opponent was frustrating him playing Michael Chang style tennis and getting every shot back continually frustrating Jeremy's player who kept trying to beat his opponent by just hitting winners from the baseline. Jeremy suggested he try something new and reminded him that in the match before this one in the doubles he won, he was volleying and returning well. Jeremy suggested in the next game in which his player was returning that he chip and charge on every serve and come into the net. What did his player have to lose? His player was down in the score and frustrated. He did something to switch his mindset from negative to positive and purposeful. His player started to do that and almost won the game going to deuce several times. In retrospect, Jeremy wishes he would have suggested this strategy sooner during the match. However, the rest of the three-day team tournament the whole-body language of his player represented more of a "true grit mindset" regardless of the score. Jeremy's player was able to understand how his negative body language and his focus on variables that he could not control was only hurting his chances of winning.

Summary

What does this "True Grit" mindset do for a player? It allows the player to leave everything on the court and in so doing control one's emotions. By applying this philosophy, whether you win or lose, you know that even when you are down, you can keep focused on things you can control. This is certainly one way to be successful both on the court and in life.

Mental Myths

"Tennis is a mental game. Everyone is fit, everyone hits great forehands and backhands."
Novak Djokovic

What are mental myths? For our purposes, at this point, they include such mistaken ideas as these: *only elite tennis players deal with the mental side of tennis in matches* or this one: *if a player gets nervous during a match then he or she is not prepared.* There are many myths we could explore, but in this chapter, our focus will be on these two.

First of all, it's just wrong that only elite tennis players deal with the mental side of the game in their matches. Any tournament player, whether one who is just starting out or one who is playing in national junior tournaments, must deal with the mental side of tennis. In fact, we would argue that the players just starting out deal with the mental side more than others. We have had experience with all levels of tournament players. For players just starting out playing tournaments, going from the practice court to the match court is tough, even if the players have incorporated match-simulated training during their practices. Players just starting out have several pressures on them that spur questions like these: "What if I lose? What if I don't live up to my parents' or coach's expectations?" and many other what if questions. The seasoned tournament players have dealt with these pressures more and have been mentally trained to handle them more effectively than beginners.

What about the other myth? "If I get nervous during a match, I am not prepared." While this may be a legitimate point, let's look at music for example or anyone performing on a stage or an athletic field. The best performers or athletes will tell you they get nervous, but you can put it into two types – (a) nervous stage fright and (b) good stage fright. Jeremy remembers growing up playing the piano and that any time he had a recital, he had a choice of either nervous stage fright or good stage fright. He remembers his piano teacher and his parents, who both played the piano, letting him know it is okay to have a little stage fright because that means you are excited about playing the piece. Nervous stage fright, on the other hand, says you are nervous because you have not practiced or prepared enough.

Pete Sampras mentions this concept in his book, *A Champions Mind,* where he talks about the 1992 US Open final he lost to Stefan Edberg, "The real giveaway, I came to realize, was that I hadn't been nervous before the match. There are two kinds of nervousness in tennis: bad nervous, which can make you freeze up, play an inhibited game or choke; and good nervous, which is sign that the match you are about to play means a lot to you—a sign that you can't wait to get out there and mix it up with your opponent, even if you are not guaranteed the win."

This statement from Sampras shows that being nervous is part of the mental mindset, whether you win or lose, and it is okay to be a little nervous before a match. It just depends on how as a player you have prepared for the match.

What about if I get nervous when I am ahead? Is there something wrong with me? If I am ahead then I should not get nervous, right? The reality is when you are ahead there is a better chance that nerves will creep into your game. We can attest to this feeling. One of the hardest things to do in a match is to close it out. Why? As a player, you start thinking about more "what if?" questions: "what if my opponent starts coming back or playing better or what if I can't handle a new strategy he/she throws at me?" The problem with this is as a player you are now focusing on the items over which you have no control. The reality is you have found something that is keeping you in control of the match, and you are on your way to winning it. Any **"what if?" questions** only take you away from this focused mindset.

Summary

As a player, it is imperative that you understand what mental questions and thoughts can hold you back and which ones can help you to be successful in a match.

"Winning Only" Mindset vs. "Competitive" Mindset

> "I've missed more than 9,000 shots in my career, lost 300 games, missed the game winning shot 26 times. I've failed over and over again in my life. That is why I succeed."
> **Michael Jordan**

> "What do you do with a mistake? Recognize it, admit it, learn from it, forget it."
> **Dean Smith**

What do we mean by a "winning only mindset" versus a "competitive mindset"? First, we need to define what we mean by both. A "winning only mindset" means you view success entirely by how much you win. On the other hand, a "competitive mindset" means winning is second to knowing you trained as well as you could and gave 100% mentally, physically and emotionally on the court. Michael Jordan's quote above sums this up well. He did not let the short-term failures cause him not to pursue what he knew he was skilled at and loved doing. Shockingly Jordan was even cut from his high school basketball team as a young player but look what he went on to accomplish! Another example of this "competitive mindset" was Rafael Nadal in 2018 texting his coach to book a practice court right after winning a match at the Monte Carlo Open while only losing five games the whole match! Nadal was not just satisfied with winning the match. He cared more about playing up to his full potential. No wonder he has won so many Grand Slams! The reality of a tennis tournament that has a draw format, as opposed to a round-robin format, is that at the end of the day there is only one champion. This not meant to be a sobering or harsh thought, but something that puts things in perspective.

Which mindset do you think is better for the long term, for life and tennis? We would argue the "competitive mindset." The "competitive mindset" allows you to put variables in the right perspective. For example, if you have a "winning only mindset" you might view uncontrollable variables such as the outcome, bad line calls, wind, the opponent's playing style, the court surface, the tournament format or your seeding placement as variables you can control. However, the reality is you can't control them. If you have a "competitive mindset," you know you can't control those variables, but instead are passionate about figuring out ways to deal with those to make you as successful as possible on the court. Another way to think about it is instead of focusing on the roadblock itself you are focused on how to deal with the roadblock.

In an article in ***Forbes*** by Garret Kramer titled "8 Surprising Characteristics of Winners at the London Olympics," he mentions these points that align with the "competitive mindset" of Olympic champions.

- Winning athletes care, and don't care about outcomes at the same time;
- Winning athletes understand that competition is the ultimate form of cooperation;
- Winning athletes feel pressure and think negative thoughts;
- Olympic champions know their perceptions are created from the inside out—in other words, their state of mind at the moment will determine their experience.

Let's look now at the trauma of handling loss. How do you do it as a player? Think about a loss in the context of the two mindsets. Did you lose because of uncontrollable factors? If you are focused on how they caused your loss in a particular match, then it will be detrimental for your long-term growth as a player. It's certainly not the way champions like Roger Federer, Rafael Nadal or Serena Williams play. We sometimes had negative reactions to uncontrollable factors when we were playing junior tennis years ago, but thankfully our coaches and other important mentors in our lives helped us develop the right perspective on what we were doing on and off the court.

Jeremy remembers how one summer during his college years he was playing a match back in the Dallas, TX area in an open men's division. "I was playing a younger player who was around 17 or 18. I was feeling confident as the older and wiser player and the college player out of the two. Unfortunately, I played the match and lost. I remember coming off the court embarrassed and frustrated. While my dad was still a positive parent about the loss, letting me know I played well, I remember saying to him, 'I should have won.' My dad responded very simply and in a non-judgmental way, 'Why?' I replied, 'Well I am the older, more experienced player." My dad said, 'That is great, however, just so you know, the player you just played was practicing this summer by traveling through Europe doing various high-performance camps and playing tournaments.' My dad knew this because he was visiting with my opponent's parent while the match was going on. Being a low-positive parent, my dad was not saying this to be mean to me; he only mentioned it because I was trying to figure out how I could have lost that match. To put this comment in perspective, I had decided to do a counseling job that summer, which certainly helped me later for working with kids, but did not help keep me match-ready for that tournament. That moment reminded me that no win is ever guaranteed in tennis."

Wins only come from knowing the process and believing in it. So, if you lose a match, make sure you know what you are reflecting on in terms of moving forward. Do some serious and honest self-reflection. Analyze what exactly went wrong and what your game plan is for correcting it. Was it the process or the factors you have no control over that you were focused on? If you always focus on uncontrollable factors, your tennis career will become a long and frustrating journey. Jeremy's experience in the story mentioned above heightened for him the importance of a competitive mindset for dealing with losses.

Let's look at another scenario. We have had players we lost to several times in a row. What serious tennis player has not faced opponents like this? It can even happen to Federer and Nadal although not very often. In our own experiences losing to the same opponents, did we quit tennis just because we lost to them several times? No, because we used the theory of incremental gains. What does this mean? It means that after losing, you identify one area you can improve to give yourself a chance to win the next match. Jeremy remembers when he started playing the open division shortly before going off to compete in varsity college tennis, there was a gentleman he played several times in the open division draw. After the first time he played him, he realized he needed to improve his return of serve because the guy had an excellent serve and volley style of play. While he never beat this player, he took joy in the fact that every time he played him he inched closer and closer to winning. The reason for his increased success was that he focused on a skill he could improve instead of complaining that his opponent's style of play was too good for him to handle. This realization helped him immensely during his college playing days.

How does all this apply to winning? Everyone loves to win, but what does it mean for you? If you are more of the "winning only mindset," then there is no more to talk about. You won the match, so you are satisfied. However, the "competitive mindset" goes a little further. It goes back to the process and example of Nadal wanting to find a practice court right after winning one of his matches at the Monte Carlo Open in 2018. For those of us with a "competitive mindset," if we win, especially in a close match, we like thinking about what strategy we used to win or how we changed something to come back. This "competitive mindset" creates a healthy player philosophy, which allows you to reflect on winning and losing in productive and positive ways.

Summary

In the end, all players must decide for themselves which mindset they want to employ in their matches as well as their preparation for tournament competition. However, we believe that the "competitive mindset" is the better route to take for both your long-term tennis journey and your life.

Point 2
Healthy Environment

Playing for the Right Reasons

"Never let the fear of striking out keep you from playing the game."
Babe Ruth

Why do you play tennis? What are your motivations? Is it for fame, fortune or fun? If it is for fame or fortune, we want to make something clear. Yes, both are possible in tennis but **not easy to come by.** This is not meant to be harsh, but "fun" should be more of a reason to play than the other two. Sure, Roger Federer is famous and has won a lot of prize money but it all started with him having fun, and he still has fun!

While we will admit we certainly cared a great deal about winning matches early on as juniors and thought that was the only reason to play, we continued to learn that it should never be the primary reason. If winning is the only reason you play, you will set yourself up for a long road of disappointments. This is not to say that players shouldn't step on the court wanting to excel at what they do. It's what all the greats have done and do— Rod Laver, Pete Sampras, Steffi Graf, Serena and Venus Williams, Rafael Nadal, Roger Federer and others. However, all the greats had a process that brought them to greatness. That's the message of this book. They all knew how to play for the right reasons that for them began with a healthy environment encouraging them with the right motivations to play. Without this, it is tough to have an enjoyable long-term career playing tennis at any level. We, fortunately, had a healthy environment presented to us to enjoy the game through our parents, mentors, and coaches at all levels. In fact, we talk about that relationship with our parents specifically in the next chapter. They helped us play for the right reasons and helped us ask the right questions.

For example, here's one. Why do we do anything in life? The answer is simple! Because we choose to, or because we are pressured to, or because it is mandatory. Where does playing tennis fall for you? Playing tennis can sometimes fall into all three of the above categories and not for any fault of the player, coach or parent. In fact, it is fair to say that any great tennis player will be able to look back positively and identify times where he/she played tennis under each of the three scenarios. The journey is filled with navigation, and that means as players we grow and evolve. Therefore, we should always ask ourselves why we play tennis at all. And why we continue to play.

The key is to start playing because you are curious—curious about the experience, the game, the beauty and the chance to have fun while playing a great sport. Tim reflects on why he got into tennis in the first place: "My own experience and the reason why thirty years later I remain strongly in the tennis world is that I started to play out of curiosity and because it was fun. This simple exposure to the game and personal reflection at a young age then led to a healthy obsession for a sport that I knew early on would be in my life in some form or another forever."

In reflecting on his junior journey, Tim says, "As my journey as a five-year-old with a love for the game morphed into that of a serious junior that would look to become a college player and maybe even a pro, the love for the game never waned. However, what did happen was that tennis became a serious part of my existence and my families. It became a part of my identity that would lead me to achieve high school and college scholarships, sponsorships from major companies and to travel throughout Europe and the United States. This reality meant that there was greater pressure and expectation. It is important to recognize the transition that an aspiring junior player will experience. When I was five, I went to my first tennis camp for a day. The day became a week, the week became the whole summer, and I was hooked! There was not one day that summer that I genuinely didn't enjoy every single moment of tennis. I would wake up, racquet in hand, and demand that my mother drive me to the club. When the camp was done, I could be found still hitting the ball against the wall. At this point in the junior pathway, it is evident that the purity of why I played tennis was not in question."

Jeremy remembers his junior journey as well: "While most of my tennis and learning as a child and junior play was done in Dallas, Texas and throughout junior camps in Texas, my first exposure to tennis started in Richmond, VA at 18 months of age when my parents hung a Nerf ball in the house and gave me a racquetball racquet to whack it as much as I wanted. The simple reality is while I was too young to remember that, I have several pictures of me growing up holding that racquetball racquet with a big smile on my face. So, when we moved to Texas when I was five years old, I always loved going to tennis camps as a kid and doing anything involved with tennis." One can readily see from both our backgrounds that two things existed early on—success for our ages and fun! Those certainly form the foundation that keeps junior players going and growing in tennis.

However, along the journey and as you grow and develop as a young player, the game transitions in the experience between wanting to play, being pressured to play and it being mandatory to play. To make sure that we stay on track and continue to play for the right reasons, we want to offer the following advice.

Being pressured to play tennis by coaches or parents when you resent it leads to an unhealthy situation and one that must be addressed no matter how difficult. On the other hand, being encouraged to play because you need guidance from people who care about you and want you to do more than spend all your time on social media or television are worth listening to because very often their guidance is warranted, and what is happening is just a natural learning curve that all young aspiring athletes go through. Tim looks back and is very grateful that his parents were wonderful letting him "do his thing" in tennis. However, he admits that he would have benefited from them being more demanding and his tennis might have improved and matured earlier if he had had a fuller understanding of the time and the commitment involved. We both believe that both parents and players should discuss their journey with people who have already lived it, mentors who can help them navigate the emotional, physical, financial and time-consuming process of playing a competitive sport as a junior.

Playing because it is mandatory means you are fully engaged in tennis as your sport and you are aware of the needs and requirements of time, money, effort and dedication to reach your potential. Your schedule inevitably becomes more set and rigid which allows you as a junior player to develop fully. This is an excellent situation on one condition—that the mandatory requirements are reasonable. What we mean by this is there are many examples where coaches and parents create the compulsory schedule, but the reality is that it is too much and not well thought through enough to allow for periodization with the performance. More importantly, it doesn't create a healthy and adequate work/life balance. This can create a negative training environment and eventually lead to physical and mental burnout. We have seen this happen too many times where coaches and parents don't see the big picture and put young athletes in adverse environments that unfortunately become a recipe for failure, resentment, and disdain for the game for life.

It's important at this point to examine the vicarious nature of parenting and coaching. There is no doubt that parents and coaches can live vicariously through, experience and enjoy the pathway of being a junior tennis player. However, like overeating ice cream there needs to be a healthy balance. If the parent is nose to the glass, sweating and stomping around at tournaments, then we have a problem. Parents who read this book, please do your kids a favor and be what we call "Passive Leaders" or "Low Positive Parents" (as we discussed in our first book, **The Complete Coach**) in your kids' lives. Kids don't need the added pressure that comes when parents cannot strike a healthy balance between passive leadership in your kid's life and an unnatural vicarious obsession.

Remember, tennis is a sport, a game, a chance to sweat, run and jump. At its purest, it is a beautiful, technical and strategic tapestry that must be enjoyed through initially a curiosity and then a love for the game. If this genuine love and appreciation for the sport exists, it will often allow the young player to navigate many of the pitfalls of a long and successful junior career and beyond.

We are happy to admit as coaches that to this day that we still love to hit balls, be on the court, go to tournaments and enjoy the process of our students both winning and losing. You can pursue a multitude of sports options as a youngster. Make sure you play the game that makes you the happiest. If you are happy doing something, then your focus and attention to developing and mastering the craft will be heightened and lead you to levels of performance and mastery that will be very satisfying all your life.

Now that we have discussed playing for the right reasons, we will examine why we have continued to play. Our reasons for playing tennis involve the following areas: **social, mental, emotional, intellectual and physical.**

Social

Friendship – Some of our best friends in life have certainly come through tennis. Our shared passion for tennis is one main reason we keep in touch with friends throughout the country and world.

Respect for Others – We have learned the importance of respecting others through tennis. This respect has taught us values such as sportsmanship, fairness on the court, and appreciating the ability of others.

Learning from Others – One of the ways we have gotten better on the court, especially in doubles, has come keeping an open mind and knowing that other players can also teach us important skills.

Inclusion – Growing up playing on high school and college tennis teams we learned the importance of diversity and the inclusion of everyone on the team, regardless of background. In the end, as a team, we had the same vision and goals during the season.

Leadership – We would not have certain leadership skills if not for our tennis. As captains and leaders on our high school and college teams, we learned valuable lessons about modeling proper behavior on the court with both actions and words, respecting teammates and serving as an example of inspiration for the whole team during times of stress during the season.

Mental/Emotional/Intellectual

Problem Solving – This is a primary skill we learned from tennis. When we were behind in the score, sensing that our strategy was not working, our opponent was making bad line calls, or we had to deal with unfavorable weather conditions, knowing how to adjust and problem-solve was crucial. Later, we devote a whole chapter to this aspect of tennis.

Positive Self-Esteem – Tennis is truly a sport that teaches the importance of self-esteem, especially during a match. We quickly learned in our match play that a major way to handle setbacks or stresses started with positive self-esteem about oneself and one's abilities on the court. This translated into resiliency and controlling one's emotions during tough mental moments on the court.

Individual Accountability and Teamwork – When we played high school or college tennis, we learned that playing both singles and doubles meant you were responsible for your own actions in your matches and equally accountable for how that affected the team's overall performance.

Resiliency – Throughout this book we suggest that resiliency is an important quality that serves as the core attribute of any champion, especially in tennis.

Math – Geometry is a huge part of tennis. There are endless games you can play and ideas you can offer to combine geometry and tennis in a fun way. We know this is true in any sport, but we think there is something unique about the way tennis can incorporate learning math in a fun way for juniors. Players need to know that winning a point is often based on understanding the geometry of the tennis court, and how hitting the ball in certain directions, and positioning yourself in certain places leads to a formula for winning every time, whether in singles or doubles.

Physical

Agility, Balance, and Coordination – These are athletic core competencies that every tennis player needs. In fact, they are considered the ABCs of athletic ability in tennis. All the athletic training we did for tennis included *agility, balance, and coordination* as the foundations, which we will discuss later in the book. We both remember participating in numerous fun games during cross training with our coaches to help us be more athletic movers on the court. This is particularly relevant today with the term "playing" sometimes referring to video games on an iPad or other devices, and not a strenuous athletic activity. Growing up in Dallas, TX Jeremy remembers in one of his junior tennis programs how each week a trainer from the NFL Dallas Cowboys team would come and lead crossover training exercises working on *agility, balance, and coordination* as part of the tennis training program. As mentioned earlier, we are excited to have Dean Hollingworth, a world-class expert, speaker, and author on this topic, offer valuable advice on training later in the book.

Endurance – While tennis is a fast burst sport, it is also an endurance sport. If you make it to the pro level, you will understand this critical feature of our sport. We both remember how many of our 2 out of 3 set matches as juniors were often very long. Thank goodness we both had endurance as part of the physical side of our junior training programs. Jeremy remembers during junior training in Dallas, TX two days a week running through the neighborhood with the other juniors in Indian run sprint fashion for 20 minutes as part of his training. Why is endurance so important? It's simple. Once you get to the final set of a match, it means that you and your opponent are even technically, so the most significant factor for winning the match, in addition to tactics, is being in shape and a mindset and will to win.

Nutrition and Fluid Replacement Awareness – Tennis helps us understand which food groups fuel us best to perform athletically on the court. Also, tennis helps us understand which meals are best for our body the night before matches. Jeremy remembers when playing a tournament in Lubbock, Texas losing a three-set match because of a poor eating choice he made for lunch before the match. Tennis also helps us know more about fluid replacement and good hydration habits before, during and after practice or match play. It helps us identify the differences in sports drinks and water regarding carbohydrates and electrolytes. We are not experts on this subject. However, if we had never played tennis, we would not have the appreciation for this topic or at least some of the understanding we have of it today.

Later in the book, we devote a whole chapter to proper nutrition written by Dr. Charlotte Alabaster, who is an expert on the subject. We encourage all players, coaches, and parents to be aware of proper nutrition and fluid replacement guidelines and take advantage of the resources out there on this topic. Information on nutrition provided by the USTA or the USTA player development is also an excellent place to start.

Stretching – Tennis has taught us the importance of both dynamic and static stretching before and after a match or practice. We believe this is not emphasized enough but should be.

Heat Illness Knowledge – Playing and teaching tennis has taught us about the causes, symptoms, and treatments for heat cramps, exhaustion, and stroke. The best junior players acquaint themselves with this information and are supported by their parents and coaches as they learn it.

Good Sleeping Habit Awareness – In our training growing up, we both learned the importance of getting enough sleep as juniors especially during the week before a tournament.

Summary

We hope this chapter has helped you understand better the reasons for playing the sport in a positive way.

Parental Pressures

"When I was young my uncle said to me, if you throw your racquet I will stop coaching you. He said that I should treat my racquet with respect because there were people in Africa with very little money who would love a racquet like mine, and that if I make a bad shot, it is my fault - not the racquet's.
Therefore, I should not take out my failings on the racquet."
Rafael Nadal

"The problem today is that if you ask a father if he'd prefer to see his son become Roland Garros champion rather than a well brought up kid, he'd choose the first option."
Toni Nadal, Rafael Nadal's Uncle and former Coach

"I'm just happy they (my kids) play tennis, and we can play as a family, and they can play with their friends one day. This is not about becoming professional tennis players, if they do that I will support it. I just want them to play sport,stay active and go out there with their friends and have fun. They are doing that, and that is wonderful."
Roger Federer

In the above quote, Federer was responding to Jim Courier in an interview after one of his wins at the 2018 Australian Open. Courier had asked Federer about his kids and their tennis. Wow! What a humble and down to earth reply from possibly the greatest player of all-time! At least from this statement, we see Federer is taking the approach of being a low-positive parent, a principle we discussed in our first book, **The Complete Coach.** Later in the book, you will see how this also relates to the principles of being a **Parent FIRST** which Lisa Goodman Stone names in her chapter on Healthy Parent-Child Relationships. As a young and aspiring tennis player, many pressures will exist, some external some internal. However, in our experience, there is nothing greater than the pressure that parents can place on a young player, intentionally or unintentionally. Junior players need to acknowledge that they are the children of parents who brought them into the world. Their parents fed, clothed, loved and supported them, and at an early age they learn and continue to respect that.

There are two different types of parents: (1) those who know they are applying pressure and (2) those who don't know. As former top junior players ourselves and now long-time coaches, we have seen it all through the years—the good and the bad. The reality is that tennis is a sport that can bring families together, but it can also tear them apart if they are not aware of some basic principles. For example, we have seen kids that were ranked at the top of the junior game going on to play college tennis for Division I schools but then stopping tennis the minute their college careers were over.

Now a warning to any parents reading this section. Be careful about requesting your kids move up too soon to the next ball progression or class. We only say this because we have seen the adverse effects that pushing has on your child. Here is our advice on the topic.

If you feel your child should move up to the next level of play (like from red to orange ball) always talk with the child about it before just deciding it. We have seen too many times where the child is just thrown into a new class at a higher level of play, and the child has no fun or success in the class. So, if you talk with your child and the child agrees that he/she would like to move up then talk to the coach. This next step is critical and speaks to the professionalism of the coach. The decision for a coach to say yes to this request should be based on one primary factor – the child is ready mentally, physically and technically. If the answer is no in any of these areas, the child should not move up. If the answer is yes in each of these three areas, then the answer we believe is yes. If there are cons to this decision, a coach should be honest about them. This way if as a parent, you and your child are insistent about the child moving up, then you are aware of potential pitfalls.

For this situation, parents and children must figure out what works best for them with advice from the coach.

Even though we come from two entirely different parts of the world (Great Britain and Texas), we have learned that the tennis journey for a junior player is based on key principles including *playing for the right reasons, acknowledging your parents' efforts, being guarded by reflection, and listening to what your parents have to say*.

First, if you are a junior tennis player, you must play because the sport gives you great joy knowing that each day you wake up with a thirst to play the game. If you as a junior are the one driving the train, then that will mean that the parents become passengers on the junior tennis journey and never doubt your passion and application. We can both confidently say any practice, travel, or training we did was based on our passion for playing, supported and encouraged by our parents, but never pressured.

Second, as a junior tennis player, you must recognize the time and investment that comes with playing junior tennis. Also, you must be aware that even as you get better or improve your ranking further for potential college coaches, your parents are investing in you because they love you first. It doesn't by any stretch of the imagination mean that the journey will be easy and that every situation will be the same. However, open your young eyes early to the sacrifice, money and time that parents invest in you to play junior tennis and to potentially reach the college or even pro level. Gratitude will go a long way toward overcoming all the swings and roundabouts that exist within the broader spectrum of the junior tennis pathway. We wish that we had said thank you more often to our great tennis parents and many others who encouraged us along the journey. Appreciation goes beyond tennis; it is about being cognizant of what people are doing for you in support of your dreams.

Third, you must be guarded by reflection. I (Tim) remember when my sister to my parents said at the age of 15 that she wanted to focus on school and time with friends. They were disappointed, but they were parents first and respected her wishes and supported her in her opinion and continued endeavors. I (Jeremy) remember when my younger brother, entering high school, initially started playing on the high school tennis team but later realized his true passion was acting. While he had more natural talent in tennis than I did, he started pursuing high school theatre more. My parents respected his decision and supported it. It turned out to be a good decision by my parents because today he is an accomplished actor doing his own one-man critically acclaimed shows around the world, making it in the entertainment business on stage, TV, and film, and still plays tennis with my daughter and me when we see him. He never lost his love for the game. That's how it should be. If you don't want to play, then let your parents know that you don't. We fully appreciate how hard this can be. However, honesty in the relationship between you and your parents is crucial at this stage in your life. The reality is that when we get serious about tennis the goal is always a college scholarship or to be #1 in the world and this level of expectation is great. Having dreams and aspirations is good. However, like all successful people in life, we need to be able to pivot when reality and expectation set in. There is not a single failed junior tennis player who doesn't look back and wishes he/she had pivoted when the writing was on the wall so he or she could experience other things, be honest with him/herself, parents and coaches. This may sound defeatist, but it isn't. The facts don't lie. The truth is that under 5% of high school athletes, both men and women, ever have the opportunity to play at the NCAA level, and only a tiny percent of those ever make it to the pro tour. It's doesn't mean you should give up on your dreams but be honest with yourself and understand when it is time for tennis to stop being the driver and become a passenger in your life journey. Trust us, in the end, you will be much happier and will enjoy tennis for a lifetime in so many other capacities.

  As a father of a young player, I (Jeremy) remember when recently my daughter Maggie had to choose between going to a birthday party for her friend or playing in a tournament to make sure her ranking did not drop a couple of points. Thankfully, with the help my wife reminding me she was only seven years old and the fact that she had could play in many more tournaments, it was better she went to the birthday party. I am glad I was able to put things in the right perspective (with my wife's help) to give my daughter a better chance of enjoying tennis as a lifetime sport.

Fourth, listen to what your parents have to say. My (Tim's) mother jokes regularly about the decisions now as a 35-year-old that I make and how she reminds me of how she gave the same advice years earlier and I resisted. The reality is that experience is more important than anything in the process of junior tennis and more importantly in life. If as a junior player, you can listen and take solace in your parents' own experiences and their guidance and advice, this will only help you and lead to a more harmonious relationship. As teaching pros and career tennis coaches, we see first-hand how kids and parents interact. There is no doubt we both were blessed with understanding parents who accepted that we weren't perfect. We would be lying if we didn't have regrets over how we appreciated what they did for us in the moment, how they picked us up when we were down and spent hard earned money on our dreams.

Parental pressures come in many shapes and forms, both on and off the court. The parent must recognize the pressures, knowing it's not easy. Our prescription is to elevate the understanding of junior tennis players, so they will respect and listen to their parents and be able to take ownership and navigate the best ways to be mutually successful. As you begin the exciting journey of junior tennis, always come back to the importance of these four fundamental principles – *playing for the right reasons, acknowledging your parents' efforts, being guarded by reflection and finally listen to what your parents have to say.*

Summary

The journey is filled with trials and tribulations, but the navigation is what is most important. You are dealing with people and expectations, the balance of which can often lead to strife. Both juniors and parents need to be honest with one another, take time to listen and at the end of the day love and care for one another. We love tennis, but we love our parents and our families more. It's all about perspective.

In the next chapter, we are excited to have Lisa Goodman Stone, a recognized expert in this field offer sound advice on the Healthy Parent/Child Tennis Relationship. She is a parent of a tennis player herself and runs the parentingaces.com website, which does a phenomenal job of posting articles and creating wonderful discussions on navigating junior development, competition and college recruiting.

Healthy Parent/Child Tennis Relationship

Lisa Goodman Stone

Going through the Junior Tennis Journey with your child can be one of the most rewarding experiences you will ever have as a parent. It can also be one of the most harrowing and can leave you both wondering why you ever thought this tennis thing was a good idea in the first place!

Being a Tennis Parent is tough. You are asked – and expected – to drive your children to lessons and drills then come back and pick them up several hours later. You are asked – and expected – to pay for said lessons and drills. You are asked – and expected – to take your children to tournaments and team events. You are asked – and expected – to ensure your children are getting the proper nutrition, off-court coaching, and mental training necessary to help them reach the highest level of the sport. You are asked – and expected – to learn and understand the college recruiting process if that's where your children aspire to play.

Your child's "winner up the line" makes you want to jump up and down with giddiness. When she closes out a match over a higher-ranked player, it feels like the best thing that could ever happen to you. At the same time, you experience every missed forehand, every double fault, and every squandered break point as though you were the one on the court fighting and competing.

You know intellectually that you must keep all those emotions inside. You are expected to sit courtside with a calm, blank expression on your face and swallow every urge to cheer or curse while your child plays. The match and its outcome are entirely out of your hands. But often your heart takes over, and you can't help yourself. Learning how to keep those emotions under control is a skill that most Tennis Parents work to develop over time just as your Player must develop his serve and slice backhand.

Doing the work, though, is the best way to maintain a healthy relationship with your child. It's tough but doable! We are here to offer you a bit of guidance as you strive to become a better Tennis Parent.

Be the Parent FIRST

The Tennis Development Pathway can be viewed as a triangle with three distinct sides: Player, Coach, and Parent.

In the equilateral version of this triangle, all three components contribute equally toward the player's ability to reach his/her tennis goals. Each person has specific duties and responsibilities, and if one fails, then the whole triangle collapses in on itself. With young or new players, the equilateral formula is necessary, sort-of a checks-and-balances system if you will. Each must hold the others accountable for holding up his or her side.

As a developing player, the player's duties include showing up for practices with a good attitude, working hard while he's on the court, doing his homework and maintaining good grades, and getting enough sleep. They also include making the hard choices—Homecoming or practice? Thanksgiving with family or an important tournament? High school party or getting a good night's sleep?

The coaches' duties include teaching the technical and tactical parts of the game, keeping the young player motivated to continue playing by making practices productive and fun, guiding the tournament schedule, being accessible to answer questions and stoke the fire, and observing tournament matches now and then. They also include showing the player the life lessons of tennis such as focus, determination, goal-setting, and fair play.

The parents' duties include all the tasks listed at the beginning of this chapter. However, you also must continue to be Mom or Dad and resist being Coach - after all, you are already paying someone you trust to fill that role. You must love unconditionally, after a win and after a loss, all the time.

As your junior player gets older, your role in the child's tennis becomes more secondary. You become a shorter side of the triangle with more of the strength coming from the player herself. That said, you are still the Parent and still a very crucial part of your child's overall development. Therefore, it is imperative that you find a way to keep your child's tennis compartmentalized and don't let it permeate life off the tennis court or outside the gym. Make sure that home is a haven away from the stresses of tennis and that you create opportunities for your family to have conversations and engage in activities that don't center on how practice went or last weekend's tournament results.

What if you are both Parent and Coach? That's where things become especially tricky. It is crucial that you find a way to be Coach *only* when you are at practice or a tournament with your child and to be Parent everywhere else. After all, you can always find another coach to work with your child, but you are the only parent (other than your partner or spouse) he has.

Let the Coach "coach"

Tennis Parents often get a bad rap from Tennis Coaches. Whether it's interfering during lessons or peppering the coach with questions at all hours of the day and night, Parents need to respect the Coach's space. If you have chosen a USPTA or PTR certified coach for your child, know that coaching comes with a certain level of knowledge and training. The more experienced the coach, the more extensive the knowledge.

You have presumably done your homework and researched the coach you've chosen to work with your child. Therefore, trust the coach and let her do her job. Just as you would never dream of telling your surgeon how to perform a surgery, you should afford your child's coach that same degree of respect. The coach is a professional and should be treated – and compensated - as such.

You must set the example for your child, too. If your child sees and hears you bad-mouthing the coach or treating her with disrespect, that may translate into how the child treats the coach as well. It can also lead to conflict between you and your child, especially if your child feels a special connection to the coach. Try to avoid any negative talk about the coach in front of your child. If you do have a concern or issue, speak to the coach privately and try to resolve it out of your child's earshot. Your child should feel that you and her coach are both on her team working together to help her reach her highest potential.

Around the Dinner Table

As the parent, you need to create a safe space for your tennis-playing children and the rest of your family. The dinner table should be one such space. Do your best to avoid talking about tennis during family meals. Your child spends enough time thinking and talking about her sport. Once she's done with practice or competition for the day, she needs to have a break from it, so respect that need and make any Tennis Talk off-limits during mealtime. Even if your child brings it up, redirect the conversation away from tennis.

Along those same lines, encourage your tennis player to pursue interests away from tennis. Playing an instrument, joining a club at school, doing community service – these are all great activities that will help your child form an identity that doesn't only center on Tennis Player. Plus, it will give you plenty of topics for discussion at mealtime.

Follow your Child's Lead

When you are spending the amount of time and money it takes to develop a tennis player, it is easy to become consumed with what the child is doing day in and day out to improve. Every time you have a moment with your child, the temptation looms large to ask how lessons are going or to discuss his latest ranking. You will be much better served to fight that temptation and let your child be the one to bring up the topic of tennis. If you are constantly talking about how practice went or what happened during last weekend's tournament, you are likely to drive a wedge between you and your child.

If your player asks your opinion on a match or whether he should go to a tournament, have the conversation. That said, you need to be careful to answer only the questions asked. Don't use your child's question to open a larger discussion around tennis. Given that so many young athletes quit their sport by the age of 13 due to burnout or other developing interests, the best gift you can give your child is to avoid over-saturating them with tennis when you are together. Let your child take ownership of his tennis and let him drive the process.

Keep him always wanting more rather than always wishing for a break from the sport. Work with his coach and come up with a training and tournament schedule that allows for some time away from the court. Try to plan those breaks around a fun school or family event such as Prom or a Spring Break vacation. You will likely find that your child returns from these planned breaks reinvigorated and ready to work hard to reach the next milestone. If you find the opposite to be the case, it may be time to have that hard conversation about whether your child is still enjoying his sport or is ready to move onto something different. Taking a few months off could be the best way to ensure he stays engaged and interested in the long-term. It could also be the best way to ensure your relationship with your child stays positive.

Before a Tournament

In the days leading up to a tournament, your child is likely feeling some pressure and stress about competing. Maybe he is facing a friend in the first round. Perhaps he must play the top seed. Maybe he IS the top seed.

Your job here is to alleviate that stress as best you can:
- Do not look at your child's draw. If you can't help yourself, then don't talk about the draw with or around your child. Some players prefer knowing ahead of time whom they will play, while others prefer to arrive at the match with no knowledge of their opponent. Your child and his coach should be the ones who decide whether to look at the draw and discuss it ahead of time.

- Teach your child to do his laundry then guide him as needed to wash everything he will wear for the duration of the tournament.
- Make sure you have your child's preferred snacks and drinks readily available for him to pack.
- Do not constantly ask your child if he has everything he needs. Ask once then leave it up to him to make sure he has his shoes, racquets, grips, water bottle, first aid kit, and so on. You are giving your child ownership of his tennis, an important step in maintaining that positive Parent-Child relationship.
- If you must travel and stay overnight at the tournament, make sure you arrange a hotel or housing well in advance and leave plenty of time to drive to the tournament site. There is no worse feeling than worrying about being defaulted from a match because you didn't arrive in time.
- As an adjunct to the point above, map out directions to the tournament site as well as to practice courts, so you aren't stressing out the morning of the event.

During a Tournament

When your child is playing a match, she wants you there, but she doesn't want you cringing or gasping or shaking your head with each point. Moreover, she certainly doesn't want a lecture right after she walks off the court, especially after a tough match. Give your child some time to calm down, to process what just happened, and to have some emotional time alone to recover. Use that time for your child to rest, shower, eat, drink, and prepare for her next match.

Once tournament play is finished for the day, try to plan something non-tennis-related to do. Visit the local zoo or amusement park. Go to a movie. Spend some time at an interesting museum. For older players, let them arrange some time to hang out with their friends at the hotel or a restaurant nearby.

If college tennis is among your child's tennis goals, you can also use the time before or after matches to take unofficial visits to local college campuses. Remember: this time with your child is a gift and passes all too quickly. Use tournament time, especially when you must travel away from home, to create special memories that will stay with you and your child for years to come.

The Ride Home

At the end of a "good" tournament, the ride home is usually pleasant. Your child may be happy to talk about his matches and his opponents. He may want to relive some of his winning shots or tell you about new friends he made. You are probably feeling pretty good, too. After all, it's fun to watch your child play well and win, and if you've done your job well, you've been holding in all those emotions for a few days and are happy to let your child hear your excitement. But what about when the tournament doesn't go so well for your child? That ride home can be miserable.

As a parent, you can be the greatest source of comfort for a player after a loss, or you can be a player's worst nightmare. No one can make a player feel better than a parent who knows how to separate their disappointment in their player's result from their role as the player's most important support system. Following a loss in a tournament (or even a tough practice), do your best to hold back any impulses you may have to analyze their play or provide your critique of what went wrong. Even when intended to be helpful, no player wants to relive a loss they just experienced. Instead, do what you do best as a parent: provide your player with support and comfort. Give your player the time and space to recover from the physical and emotional exertion of competition. And ice cream, ice cream always helps!

The challenge is to temper your emotions whether it's a good tournament or not so good. You don't want your child ever to feel like your love for him is based on winning and losing. Work to avoid over-gushing after a win and over-stewing after a loss. It's just tennis, and your child's feelings – as well as your relationship with him – are far more important.

Look Beyond the Tennis

Your player, throughout her career, will do plenty of worrying about forehand net errors, first serve percentages, and dropped match points. As a parent, take pride in having the wisdom to see the big picture. Our sport provides endless life lessons for a young player, and it is the parent who has the perspective and wisdom to highlight these moments for a player to learn who comes out of the Tennis Journey with the relationship with his child intact. Facing and overcoming adversity, the art of hard work, handling disappointment, coping with pressure, developing goal-setting skills, the ability to be successful on her own - the list of Life Skills tennis teaches is endless. Your child will never remember that first-round loss when she was 13 at that local tournament or that double fault on match point when he was 9, and neither will you. What your child will remember is the lessons you helped to teach through their experiences with tennis, and that you were there for the entire journey.

Lisa Stone Bio

Lisa Stone is the creator of ParentingAces, a website, and podcast for junior and college tennis parents and coaches. A graduate of UCLA, Lisa Stone is a Mom who also happens to be a Tennis Mom (or Tennis Zealot, as one friend calls her). As the former Chair of the Georgia Governor's Commission on Physical Fitness & Sports and President of Fit For 2, Inc., Stone has been involved in the fitness and sports arena for over 25 years. Stone has been playing tennis her entire life though never at the level her youngest child reached. Through ParentingAces.com and the ParentingAces Podcast, Stone shares what she's learned about navigating the Junior Tennis Journey and College Recruiting with other parents and coaches who are hungry for her insights and knowledge. She is available for speaking engagements, tournament consulting, and college recruiting guidance. You can reach Stone via email at lisa@parentingaces.com.

The Power of Low Positive Parenting

Dr. William J. Carl III

Okay, I admit it, I love tennis so much that as soon as our older son, Jeremy, could stand on his own two feet I put a racquetball racquet in his tiny hands, hung a tennis ball from the doorway by a string between our large entryway and our dining room and said, "Hit it, Jeremy, hit it!" Poor kid just stared at me. When he did give it a try and missed, I said, "Keep your eye on the ball!" at which point he took the ball and placed it directly on his left eye. I love how kids are so literal about everything.

Amazingly, he went on to be an NCAA All-American and Captain of his college tennis team at Presbyterian College in Clinton, South Carolina. Later, after working several years at The White House, Jeremy became a full-time teaching pro coaching at Regency Sport and Health Club in McLean, VA, the Arlington, VA and Bethesda, MD YMCA tennis programs, has served as Director of Tennis at one of the nation's major tennis clubs in Washington, DC, Mt. Vernon Athletic Club in Alexandria, Virginia, and is now a teaching pro at Belle Haven Country Club.

Jeremy was chosen as one of only 48 coaches worldwide (every two years) to participate in USTA's prestigious High Performance Coaching Program in Boca Raton, FL. Having completed that elite training program in January 2015, he has been certified by the USPTA as a Specialist in Competitive Player Development. He's also been selected for other High Performance Coaching programs at 2016 Indian Wells, CA and during the 2016 Davis Cup matches in Portland, OR and the 2017 Davis Cup matches in Birmingham, AL. He was also named USPTA Tennis Pro of the Year for 2016 in the Mid-Atlantic Conference, an honor voted on by his peers, and he has reached the Elite Professional status in USPTA.

How did he make the transition? I wish I could take the credit, but the reality is Jeremy's game took off the moment I got out of the way. Oh, sure, I showed him a few things in those early years when he was little. However, at some point, I realized that, even though I'm a pretty good player myself and Jeremy was amazingly patient with all my parental exhortations and interventions, I was not the person to help his game blossom and flourish. Who helped me see that? A couple of pros in Dallas, Texas—David Redding at Northwood Country Club and Jack Newman at Fretz Tennis Center. Both of them showed me how to be a good tennis parent.

David Redding (who is now the Head Coach at Harding University in Arkansas) was giving Jeremy a lesson one day, and I was pacing the sidelines like a caged lion occasionally growling things like, "Jeremy, move your feet! Turn sideways on those overheads! Hit that ball down the line on that approach shot, not crosscourt!" At one point, David said, "Jeremy, why don't you pick up these balls; we'll hit again in a minute," then sauntered casually in my direction. I didn't even see it coming. In retrospect, I realize what a tightrope pros walk when they confront enthusiastic parents. If they turn them off, the angry mom or dad leaves the club or finds another pro that will let them yell at their kids from the sideline.

David was very gentle with me. He simply smiled and said, "Hey, Bill, why don't you take a break and go have a cup of coffee." "But," I replied, "don't you need me here, so I will know what to work on when we have practice sessions in between?" He shook his head and said something I will never forget. "It's like life, Bill. Sooner or later, you have to let him go and let tennis be something 'he' wants to do, not something 'you' want him to do. The same is true about everything in his life." Well, the proverbial ton of bricks couldn't have hit me harder. However, it was exactly what I needed to hear. I did have that 'cup of coffee,' and it was the best coffee break I've ever had.

Jack Newman is a Master Tennis Professional and now Head Coach and CEO of the Austin Tennis Academy. He and I were talking one day as dozens of Dallas' finest junior players were going through their paces in one of his famous Fretz Tennis Center clinics. We were discussing the idea of what the parents should do and not do for their children to thrive in tennis. I listened carefully since Jack has sent more teenagers on to the college and professional levels than any other pro I know. I figured he had found the secret. What he told me that day applies to parent-child relationships in every part of life and, as David Redding had indicated earlier, not just in tennis. He helped me understand that the T-Shirt shouldn't say, "Tennis is Life: The Rest Is Just Details" but instead "Life is like Tennis: Learn All You Can!"

Jack told me that day that he's observed four types of tennis parents: **High Positive, High Negative, Low Positive, and Low Negative**. He then asked me which type of parent I thought was behind his most successful juniors, in other words, the players who went on to the college and professional levels. Surely this was a trick question, and I was right, it was. My initial answer, of course, was High Positive since I figured that High Negative, the 'yelling-screaming-kicking-things,' parents would only destroy a child's fragile ego and Low Negative, the 'simmering-on-the-sidelines-frown-faced-arms-crossed,' parents would be little more than slow-drip torture for the son or daughter slugging it out on the court. Thus, it was apparent, by their names if nothing else, that High Negative and Low Negative Parents were poison for their children.

So, High Positive had to be the right answer. That was my choice, and I was sticking to it. "Is that your final answer?" said Jack. Nervously, I replied, "Yes, I'm sure of it...at least I think so...." Jack smiled, going in for the kill. Wrong, tennis ball breath!

The correct response was Low Positive. What? I needed an explanation, which Jack happily provided. High Positive parents hover way too much. They are too overly enthusiastic, always praising, always pumping their kids up, and always congratulating them when they hit a good shot or win this game or that match.

The problem comes when they don't provide the over-the-top response. Kids get so conditioned to hearing it and expecting it that when it doesn't happen, they are crushed. Or they feel bad about themselves because they have let their parents down. That's the hidden danger of being a High Positive parent.

Low Positive parents, on the other hand, are genuinely supportive but allow their children to make tennis their own. They don't watch every lesson or clinic, hanging around, exploding like High Negative parents or simmering on the sideline like Low Negative parents. Instead, they encourage but do not push. They support but do not intrude. They drop their children off for lessons and clinics then get a manicure, a cappuccino or work-out at the fitness center themselves. At the end of the lesson or clinic, they pick their children up and ask them how it went and how they felt about how they did. Even after a match, they don't judge or criticize. Again, they ask the child how the experience was for them. ONLY if the child asks for it, does a parent offer any advice at all and that in the context of genuine and straightforward affirmation.

Now, I realize on the surface this sounds like so much touchy-feely, 1970s cotton candy—lots of fluff with no substance. I mean where's the action plan for success, the strategic plan with key goals and target dates? Don't we pamper these millennial and post-millennial kids way too much as it is these days? How can your child ever improve with this lackadaisical "everybody gets a trophy" attitude from Mom or Dad? The truth is it works. Leave the performance assessment and enhancement to the professionals. After all, they're the ones trained for it. David Redding and Jack Newman are right. I observed it myself. The players in Texas whose parents ran their children into the ground burnt them out by the time they were 18, if not before.

The day I went for my famous 'cup of coffee' and became a Low Positive Parent was the day Jeremy's game took off. He went on to be the Captain of his Division II NCAA Varsity Tennis Team at Presbyterian College in Clinton, SC, helping his team win the South Atlantic Conference Championship his senior year. His coach at the time, Bobby McKee, further developed his game and his ability to teach and mentor others. And now Jeremy is a seasoned teaching pro helping me improve my game!

In addition, Jeremy and Tim have had opportunities to teach kids at the ATP/WTA Citi Open, with Wayne Bryan, the father and coach of the Bryan Brothers. He told Jeremy and Tim "the most important thing I ever did for my boys was to guide them in what makes them happy and success will follow." That's exactly what Jeremy is doing with his daughter, Maggie. I can say for sure that Jeremy has learned how to be a good tennis parent.

"Billie Jean King's early sport was softball; at age 10, she played shortstop on a team of 14 and 15-year-old girls that won the city championship. However, her parents suggested she try a more "ladylike" sport, and at age 11, she began to play tennis on the Long Beach public courts." ("Billie Jean King," Biography.com)

Once during an interview, King said the following about her parents' influence on her tennis career:

> My mom came to get me, and I jumped in the car and said, "Mom, mom, this is it, this is it." She said, "What do you mean *this is it*?" And I said, "I found what I'm going to do with my life. I'm going to be the number one tennis player in the world," And my mom goes, "You have homework, and piano." My mom kept us absolutely grounded, forever! (Interview on CBS News, Sunday Morning, September 17, 2017)

Clearly, Billie Jean King's mother was a Low Positive parent. We wonder whether that was part of the reason she was so successful. Well, it certainly didn't hurt.

So, if you are a tennis parent, and you want to make sure your children burn out or give up the game long before they reach their true potential, continue being a High Negative, Low Negative or High Positive Parent. Your kids will quit tennis faster than a John Isner serve. However, if you want your children to go to the next level and have half a chance of being the best they can be in this wonderful game, start today becoming a Low Positive Parent and watch them take off! Speaking from experience, I can tell you this—you will be glad you did.

Dr. William J. Carl, III Bio
William J. Carl III, PhD is an author, lecturer, pastor, professor, former academic president and enthusiastic amateur tennis player who wishes he was half as good as his son, Jeremy! Dr. Carl lectures on the Brain at medical schools and medical conferences and applies his knowledge of neuroscience to helping tennis players remember to be competitors who always "play smart" on the court.

What Parents and Kids Both Want from Tennis

Linda Paul

**"Ill can he rule the great that cannot reach the small."
Edmund Spenser**

One of the most rewarding aspects about coaching juniors is coming off the court with your junior student and the parent asking his/her child "How was it?" and the child responding, "It was fun!" Then the parent says to you, "Thanks for a great lesson." The reality is every parent and child are hoping for that good tennis experience from every lesson. For many coaches, this is the main motivation, certainly the first motivation for coaching kids. However, it is very easy for a coach to get caught up in seeing the kids' "potential" and start preparing them for the pro tour. As a teacher and a parent of a player who went from a young five-year-old who never could stop just hitting balls even after a day of tennis camp to a top junior player and later Division I college player in the United States, I have come to realize best practices that exist between player and coach that create a healthy environment for the tennis journey.

    The reality is the coach, the child and the parent should work as a team with each person having an important role in developing the student. The coach is the mentor for the child on his/her tennis journey. The parent is the encourager. The child should be the driver for achieving his or her goals. One philosophy that guided me as a parent was this: "Life is Like Tennis: Learn All You Can and Never Stop Learning."

    Below are the main life lessons that kids and parents are looking for from a tennis coach. They include **awareness, valuing other's time, good communication, integrity, and commitment.**

Awareness

Awareness is a vital part of what parents and children are looking for in lessons. Here are the items every coach should keep in mind:

- Coaches should be aware of the child's schedule; has the child come straight from school, is he/she dehydrated, hungry or tired?
- Does the child know what skills to practice in between lessons and how to achieve goals?
- Listen to parents, but be honest with them and base all training recommendations on a performance-based plan, not the child's "potential." This will let parents know you are interested in developing the whole player and help them better understand the process needed to achieve the child's goals and the parents' role in that process.

Valuing the Other's Time

Parents and kids are busy. So, the unprepared coach looks like the uncaring coach to both the parent and the child. The coach should respect that both the child and the parent want to get away from the regular aspects of life or need an outlet. The child and parent want the coach to know them by name. All players have similar stresses related to tennis, and the coach is there to understand the stresses and help guide both parents and children in dealing with them. Time is valuable, so coaches must be disciplined in how they use their time on the court. Coaches should always be organized, pro-active and encouraging.

Good Communication

Coaching communication is both non-verbal and verbal. 90% of effective coaching comes from non-verbal actions such as eye contact, facial communication, and body language and only 10% is verbal. When children come off the court, parents rarely ask the child first, "What was the tip you learned from the coach today?" Instead, it's always more focused on "did the child enjoy the experience and have fun?" The only way for the parent and the child to know that information is if the delivery of the lesson plan was *competent, creative and concise*. These are the three C's for creating good communication in a tennis lesson.

Integrity

Parents and children are looking for integrity in their coaches during lessons as well as in between them. Integrity builds respect as coaches model it for their students especially when it is a key feature of their teaching philosophy. One of the primary results of this philosophy is that it lets the parent and the child know one of your primary goals is to increase the player's self-esteem because self-esteem serves as the basis for any player's ability to compete.

Commitment

Commitment to helping a child reach his/her full potential as a player is a vital trait that both parents and kids expect from a coach. The effect of successfully doing this equals a sports person who participates well and spends a lifetime enjoying the sport. In mathematical terms PP+CC = CSJ (positive parent + committed coach = continuing sports journey through life for the child). There are several ways a coach can show commitment:

- Focus on learning about the player by asking these types of questions first: "What do you like about school?" "Tell me about your friends?" "What other sports do you play?" "How was the camp you went to last week?" "How was your dance recital?"
- Understanding all little things matter. Being on time, prepared 15 minutes before the lesson with all the teaching equipment out is crucial to setting the right tone for the lesson. Actively listening to the child's name the first time you meet. If the child is using the wrong size racquet, then let the parent know that the child needs to use a different racquet to ensure the child enjoys the game and develops correctly.

- Positive and Productive Words Matter. Finding the good with sentences like "You tried hard then, well done, but if you could move your feet a little quicker to short balls, it will help you be on balance to hit the shot down the line." A sentence like this will motivate the child to do better, and parents will see the respect you have for their children.

Summary

Both parents' and children's needs can be met in a lesson by making sure the following principles are addressed: **awareness, valuing the player's time, good communication, integrity, and commitment.**

<u>**Linda Paul Bio**</u>
Linda is lifelong educator and expert in child development and education. Linda is a former Principal in many schools in the United Kingdom and the owner of Education Journey. She specializes in physical education and elementary age mathematics.

A Sibling's Take

Sancha Legg

This book is a testament to the fact there is some great advice out there for coaches, players, and their parents. However, someone that is often overlooked when it comes to advice is the sibling. Whether a brother or sister, older or younger, a player or not, if a coach or parent can include the sibling in the player's journey, then it can increase participation and all the health benefits that go with it. Besides, it can also improve feedback and analytical skills, endorse teamwork, promote sibling respect and more practically provide a solution for childcare! This chapter looks at some simple considerations a coach can make to enhance the experience of the sibling and therefore the whole family unit. Everything mentioned below I experienced or witnessed myself. I was an active, younger sister to my brother, Tim, who was a very successful junior tennis player. The strong bond I share with my brother, the respect I have for his achievements and the respect he has for my opinions, were fostered through some of these simple steps.

    I will start with one I am always shocked that I don't see practiced more often: allow the sibling to sit at the side of the court during private lessons. However, I would add a caveat here that the sibling must be old enough to be able to sit by him/herself for 60 minutes and not be disruptive. As the coach, you should give the sibling an objective task like counting and noting the number of unforced errors, or balls in the net vs. balls played long. At the end of the lesson ask for the fact-based feedback. By being objective instead of subjective, the feedback will not be taken in the wrong way. The sibling has provided a service to the player and the coach and while doing so has, in very basic terms, learned analytical skills, the importance of attention to detail and more importantly a deeper investment in your player's progress. This works brilliantly with younger siblings who aspire to garner the respect of their older siblings. The younger sibling is now the analytical coach, the person with the stats and, as we all know, information is power. The sibling is now part of the team! At the dinner table that night the sister or brother can update the family on the player's progress. These lesson analytics can evolve into homework. At tournaments, simple spreadsheets can be printed off and filled in by the sibling. The sibling is entertained and not just sitting aimlessly or running around. Siblings are practicing mathematical proficiency and without knowing it learning the intricate tactics of the sport. They are being educated. Education in sport is what breeds participation and can be the simple solution to improving the gender and socio-economic gaps that sadly exist in most sports today. If siblings play the same sport themselves then they have stats to beat, mistakes to learn from and a hero to emulate.

    I was fortunate enough to go to the same school as my older brother. As any younger sibling will tell you the elder sibling sets a path which you follow (or in my case try to beat!). My brother was Head Boy, and I wanted to be Head Girl. My brother got 4 As, and I wanted 5. You can only follow the good if you witness it. My school cottoned on to this at an early stage. The older kids always sat at the front in assembly, being well behaved. We wanted to be the older kids, so we copied them. Fortunately, our sports club did the same. Tennis squads were timetabled, so the skill set above you played on the courts next to you. There was a hierarchy of skill sets and the path to success, to the top squad, was clear. I got the same feeling watching the Top Squad girls come onto the court after I'd finished, that I did watching Steffi Graf walking out onto Centre Court at Wimbledon. The cool thing was that the Top Squad was only a two-hour time slot away from me and an achievable shorter-term goal. I often think many potential champions fail because the gap between the Top Squad and being the professional is too vast. If only there were more squads in-between. If logistics deem the same time or back to back sessions impossible then why not invite younger siblings or less advanced players along to watch the top squads train? Run a five-minute feedback session at the end. Who did the spectators think tried hard? What did these players do that you don't do in your squads? Do you want to be in this squad one day? Yes! Feedback skills, tick. Goal setting, tick. A bunch of inspired youngsters, tick.

Finally, as a coach take time to find out more about the siblings of your players. What are their interests? This is vital if the sibling doesn't play the sport as well. If, however, the siblings are active, perhaps play another sport, then find training exercises that benefit both your players and their siblings' sports. Do both sports rely on hand-eye coordination? Do they both need upper body strength and stamina? Set fitness homework that can benefit the whole family. If siblings are not active, then what do they like? I remember as a child, our family getting our first camcorder and I was obsessed with making music videos. My brother's coach suggested that I film my brother playing matches. Something real to film! I have never been so excited to watch my brother play a match. I remember one of my fellow player's sisters was really into fashion design and could be seen sitting at the side of the court taking inspiration from all the players around her and sketching her latest sporty designs. Do they like to cook? How about suggesting some nutritious protein snacks for your player to try mid-match? After all, I bet they are fed up with the same old boring banana and energy drink.

It seems crazy to me that so much time and effort are put into keeping parents, players and coaches focused on creating a champion and yet a key pillar to the household is overlooked—the siblings! The steps above are small, and they take little effort, but can transform a player's experience, their relationship with brothers and sisters, and their development emotionally and educationally. Small price, big payoff. Seems worth it to me.

Sancha Legg Bio
Sancha is former top junior tennis player in the United Kingdom. She is now Executive Director – Equity Sales - at Goldman Sachs. She is a board member of the England & Wales Cricket Board (ECB) Participation and Growth Board. She is a contributor to the Women's Tennis Coaching

Association (WTCA) and holds a degree from the London School of Economics and Political Science (LSE).

Coaching Expectations

**"All coaching is, is taking a player
where he can't take himself."
Bill McCartney
Former NFL Player and Coach**

As an aspiring junior tennis player, you will be fortunate and unfortunate with the coaches who work with you. The more we can be transparent about this the better, and therefore can advise you on what to look for in a coach.

We start by thinking about our journeys. When Tim first started coaching at 22, he was young, passionate and authoritative. Jeremy, coaching at 29, was professional and prepared (and continues to be) but sometimes was too businesslike in his actions on the court which would keep his students from seeing his passion for helping them learn the game. Not necessarily bad, but also not the most effective. Both of us had a lot to learn early on. Any coach that's worth his/her salt will tell you that humility, passion, and accountability are the best ingredients.

Let's define the role of the coach: Coaches are hired, paid or volunteer to make you a better player, plain and simple. If they are showing up unprepared or are on their phones while you're doing your best to perfect your game, FIRE THEM! We have one life and one opportunity to be the best junior players we can be, so make it happen and don't let an undisciplined, unprofessional coach stop you from reaching your goals. Coaching should never be about just making money. Remember, an impressive playing background doesn't always equal impressive and passionate coaching skills. We feel fortunate to have learned how to coach well without having a Grand Slam to hang our hats on. While playing competitive and high-level junior tennis certainly helps with coaching, it sometimes doesn't help with aspects like communicating well with students and knowing the different learning styles of all kinds of players.

Coaches must also have these 12 essential qualities of a professional: **proactive, responsible, optimistic, fundamental, efficient, steady, a student of the game, introspective, observant, nurturing, adaptable, and leadership.** We will briefly describe each one.

Proactive – Good coaches always have training equipment set up and lesson plans ready before each practice; they also display other simple but important proactive traits. It starts with coaches valuing your time.

Responsible – Coaches need to be responsible with what they use to train their students. This means, for example, getting the right type of balls ready (red, orange, green, or yellow) for your training. The correct long-term development of a player should be the top focus of every coach.

Optimistic – Coaches should have the quality of seeing the positive even in negative situations. This applies to both the practice court and the match court. If you miss a shot, then the remark should not be a negative focus on the result, but instead, a performance positive on something the player did well but can improve.

Fundamental – All coaches should be passionate about teaching the fundamentals of movement, swing path, and so on, just as much as they are about teaching "higher level elite shots."

Efficient – This means valuing a player's time on the court. Coaches through passion and continuing education should be focused on doing everything possible to offer tips and strategies that will maximize the player's time.

Steady – All great coaches are steady in their interactions with players regardless of the situation. If some discussion about the player's attitude during practice or a match is warranted, coaches should approach this situation rationally and calmly when addressing the player or the parents. Remember the reason for a player's poor attitude might reflect the coach's attitude.

Student of the Game – This means that a coach is passionate about continuing education and does not assume he/she knows it all.

Introspective – The best coaches are willing to ask self-reflective questions about their coaching if players are acting up on the court or not seeming to understand coaching tips that are being delivered.

Observant – The best coaches see things others can't see when correcting a shot. An observant coach can focus specifically on what part of the shot should be improved—**footwork, backswing, contact point, forward swing or follow through.**

Nurturing – Nurturing is defined as being encouraging and caring for the growth and development of the student. This is by far one of the primary traits any coach should have.

Adaptable – We can attest that we are not perfect and sometimes need to deviate from a path we started with a student to ensure that for the long-term that student will be better served. It starts with being confident in our abilities, but also being able to admit, "We might have screwed up, and we need to fix it."

Leadership – All coaches should have the skill of leadership and be thirsty to improve every day. The reality is a coach should lead by example with positive and productive actions, directing the lesson plan once a goal is established, and being an authority on the topic to name a few. This applies to both group and private lessons.

Assume you have found that coach who sees beyond the money and any dreams of fame and fortune at the highest level and has these 12 essential qualities. If you have found a coach that values your time and the money your parents spend, then you are off to a great start because that means the relationship between you and the coach is based on respect. However, we are not finished! If you find these essential traits in a coach, you as a player must acknowledge and appreciate them because coaching done right is truly up there with nursing or teaching as one of the most selfless professions.

In addition, it's important to consider how your parents interact with the coach, which we will address in a different chapter. However, your respect for the coach who's there to help you is crucial.

Tim reflects on this part of his journey. "My parents taught me at a young age the value of having a great coach, and it helped me in my working relationship with the coaches I had. Although now a tenured coach in the U.S. myself, I see many examples where good coaches want the best for their students, and parents and juniors are not respectful of the time and skill they bring. On the flip side, I see some coaches who are merely in pursuit of a lazy paycheck." Neither represents a good model for the junior player.

As a result, we will now discuss the important attributes that all great coaches have to ensure the best coach/consumer relationship possible. Two essential attributes of great coaches are (1) they are passionate about their subject and (2) they care that their students learn. All other attributes that we will discuss in this chapter stem from these two.

One of the most significant attributes any great coach has is the ability to let students know through the respect established between player and student that all their actions are heartfelt. Jeremy remembers an instance from his time growing up with one of his coaches that serves as an example of this principle.

"I was a teenager and had a very consistent two-handed backhand. I was already involved playing junior tournaments in the championship level all over the state of Texas. One day one of my coaches said, 'I think if you switch from a two-handed to a one-handed backhand it will benefit your game overall in the long run and allow you to add more shot selection to your groundstroke making it more of a weapon.' I remember him also saying after I agreed to switch to the one-handed backhand, 'You need to use it in matches even if it means losing initially.'" And of course, I did lose a few matches as I adjusted.

Looking back on this moment Jeremy realizes that the coach modeled two critical principles – any technical tip a coach gives should be based on helping the person in the long run and let the student know how it will help specifically. In addition, the tips should not be just because it will help the student win in the short term. The winning should come from the fact that the tip helped with the overall development of the player.

We also believe a great coach should have boundless patience and be authentic in wanting to meet his/her student's goals, not the coach's goals. Let's face it, without these two qualities there is no way there can be the respect between a coach and a player that is needed for success. These two qualities also speak to the coach's love for coaching in general. Tennis coaches should love coaching first and teaching tennis second. We remember from our own experiences these are two major reasons we stayed in the game throughout our junior days and beyond.

Also, the coach should continue to learn. To be truly professional, coaches should do all they can to be current with their knowledge of their profession. For example, you expect your doctor, your lawyer, auto mechanic or your accountant to be truly professional and up-to-date, right? Why not a tennis coach? Of course, you do! While there are good coaches that may not be certified, we without any doubt have seen the huge benefit for our players in us having multiple certifications.

These ideas can be summed up from a formula in our first book: **Passionate Coach + Continued Education = Complete Player.** Our sport is constantly changing. Let's face it. Many people can give you a tip on how to hit a better shot, but **you are paying the coach for the delivery of the tip, not just the tip.** We like to put tips into two categories – **the coaching tip and the professional coaching guidance tip.** The coaching tip might be only positive and is said without any real specificity. On the other hand, a professional coaching guidance tip is both positive and specific while displaying more of a mentorship role.

While tips like "shorten your backswing on your service return" or "give more distance between you and the ball on the contact point on your groundstrokes" might be correct, ensuring that the tips are focused on empowering the student to apply them in a match is even more important. As we have learned from our USTA High Performance training, continuing education through

USPTA and PTR opportunities and our years of coaching, tips must be purposeful, helpful and body part specific.

Below are some common tips and how each one can be more purposeful, helpful, and body part specific.

Common Coaching Tips	Professional Coaching Guidance Tip
"Swing Low to High"	"On groundstrokes, swing racquet head from knee height to over the shoulder."
"Finish Your Swing"	"On the forehand, have the butt of the racquet and the elbow of your hitting arm pointing toward the other side of the court when you finish your swing."

Why else is this continuing education important? Coaches need continuing education to accurately relate to their students mentally, emotionally, technically, physically and tactically. One of our main passions for writing this book comes from our desire to continually improve our coaching. We don't know it all, but we want to know as much as we can. If any coach acts like a know-it-all, be careful. This is specifically important when helping players decide between style and substance. In this day and age of video lessons, coaches must know which video advice applies to their specific players and which doesn't apply.

Passion for coaching should involve a love for teaching the fundamentals of development. This can be applied to any person teaching a skill. Jeremy played the piano for six years when he was growing up. He remembers his piano teacher not as a piano teacher per se but as a great teacher who loved what she taught. Just like a good coach teaching a lesson well, Jeremy remembers she loved making sure he knew how to play scales correctly with each hand before combining his two hands.

Our final word of advice on this topic is to make sure your coach is fully engaged. We think this quote from Phil Jackson, 11-time NBA champion coach and former NBA player, says it best, "Winning is important to me, but what brings me real joy is the experience of being fully engaged in what I do." This is a great quote. It stresses values such as **joy, experience, and engagement in coaching**.

We like to use the "Mother Teresa Test" regarding someone who is engaged in a genuine passion or calling. Not many people can question the true reason why Mother Teresa did what she did because her actions showed she could care less about the fame she got but cared more about serving others.

Summary

We hope this chapter has advised you on how to know what should be expected of a coach, so you can find the best one possible to help you on your tennis journey and your journey through life.

High School, College or Pro – Where Will Your Journey Take You?

"Success is about having, excellence is about being. Success is about having money and fame,
but excellence is being the best you can be."
Mike Ditka

Where do you want to go with your tennis? That is the question you must ask yourself once your curiosity and initial love for the game has transpired. In life, we need to set goals—goals that are measurable and that we can be accountable to. Goals for tennis are as important as goals for school or family because they are all intrinsically linked.

Notice this chapter references four outcomes in tennis. They are to play high school, college, pro or socially with your friends. Whatever your goals for playing, make sure it involves playing for *the love of the game*. It's easy to forget *the love of the game* as you navigate the many branches of junior tennis, not to mention the health, emotional and social benefits of the sport. The good news for any young player reading this and trying to figure it out is that you have options. In fact, there are many options, all of which leave tennis in your life whether it is front and center on the pro tour or merely as a passionate hobby while you train to become a doctor or a lawyer, for example. That is the beauty of the sport! It acts as a great leveler, an excellent means of networking and self-improvement far beyond your high school, college or pros years.

We have some simple advice when it comes to figuring out where you want your tennis career to go. First, the key to any successful life is to have options. Look at this all too familiar scenario. I am a young tennis player, and all I want is to turn pro, and therefore all my focus is on that and not on school, friends, and family. Consequently, I live a very isolated existence. Of course, there are exceptions in which this single focus has worked, but if you look at most young tennis players worldwide, this is a horrible way to set goals. Ask yourself, when you graduate from high school, wouldn't you love to have multiple options like playing collegiately, turning pro or putting it on the back burner for now while you follow your dream to be a doctor, artist or musician, and let tennis become a life tool? I know which one I would choose. It is not to say you shouldn't reach for the stars in your tennis journey and that you shouldn't be obsessed with being the best you can be every time you step on a court. However, be guarded by reflection, focus on the big picture and give yourself every opportunity both in your chosen sports, academic schooling and with family and friends to achieve outcomes in all scenarios that may exceed your dreams. It is this well-rounded individual that more often succeeds in tennis and life for him or herself, family and society overall.

Let's begin with high school tennis. High school tennis is a very inconsistent product depending on where you live within the United States. You either have teams with most of the players being very serious and talented or the top two being very good and serious and the rest of the team doing it for social reasons. Jeremy remembers growing up playing junior high tennis and going all three years undefeated, never losing to any of his teammates or any matches against other schools. Even though Jeremy still had a successful high school tennis career, he did not go undefeated. However, his high school and USTA playing level helped him get recruited to a college tennis team, which we will mention later. Often underfunded programs despite some coaches' best efforts, junior high and high school coaches typically are teachers moonlighting to make a few extra dollars. Jeremy's junior high tennis coach was the assistant football coach who had been assigned to coach the tennis team but had never picked up a racquet. His high school tennis coach was his AP English teacher who did a good job coaching the team even though tennis was not a primary sport for him. However, he cared a great deal about doing the best he could as a coach.

Also, in the United States where the focus to reach the college level is on USTA and now UTR rankings, high school academics can often be a time consumer that, depending on your level and your goals, can get in the way of tennis. It is imperative that as a junior player you play high school tennis for the right reasons—the team aspect in preparation for college, the responsibility of playing and competing for something bigger than yourself in your school and your teammates. Both are vital lessons in a sport that is often very isolated and lacks the benefits of the team environment and the responsibility to "team." We would love to see high school tennis be more of a mechanism for college recruitment more like it is in Football, Baseball, and Basketball. Unfortunately, it is not so and being aware of this is vital to any aspiring college or pro player. Many of the players that we have worked with and have taken to the college ranks would play maybe their freshman and sophomore year of high school tennis and then knuckle down on the bigger goal of playing collegiately. Everyone's situation is different, and therefore you must set goals, but also have coaches, parents, and peers around you who can help keep you on track.

Collegiate tennis! The "Holy Grail" to play NCAA sports. A resume builder for you, your coaches and your parents to dine out on for a lifetime. However, what does playing college tennis mean? Well in the NCAA, NAIA system there are varying levels of collegiate tennis based typically on the size of the school and the funding the school provides for tennis. The good news is that college tennis is very broad in the level that you need to achieve a place on a team for four years. This is a good thing in that many levels and aspirations that combine the best balance of playing and studying are available. However, it is incredibly competitive, and we would be doing a disservice to our readers if we weren't honest about the declining number of collegiate programs for a multitude of reasons. We have had students academically gifted and average tennis players play at Division 1 schools where maybe funding was limited, or a coaching change had happened. We have seen highly ranked national players choose lesser tennis schools because their desired academic program has taken the front seat. Tim attended on scholarship George Mason University which is considered a mid-major NCAA Division I program because his tennis aspirations on the pro tour had begun to shift. He wanted to play in college and for it to be paid for as well as studying his passion, which was Economics. At George Mason, he was able to combine high-level tennis in what at the time was the very competitive Colonial Athletic Association against such powerhouses as Virginia Commonwealth, Old Dominion, and William and Mary with also studying near the nation's capital under two Nobel Laureates in Economics. This isn't to brag, but it goes to show how tennis and academics can go hand in hand, complementing one another.

Jeremy attended Presbyterian College in Clinton, S.C. playing on the varsity tennis team. He was captain of the team his senior year, one of the years they won their division, at the time called the South Atlantic Conference. Jeremy was on scholarship and an NCAA All-American at Presbyterian College. He also had pro tour aspirations but being realistic about those chances, tennis still gave him options to be involved in the sport and create a professional career in coaching. He was interested in going to a small liberal arts college in the Southeast and playing on a college's varsity NCAA team. Tennis provided both for him. Tennis gave him a bridge to connect with Bobby McKee, the Presbyterian College tennis coach at the time, who taught Jeremy a lot about tennis and a lot about life. Jeremy loved the camaraderie of being on the team and traveling throughout the South for matches. As we can both attest, this college tennis experience not only kept us in tennis but taught us lessons about teamwork and accountability as leaders that we have used daily in our professional life since college.

Finally, the pro tour! The glorious end game for any junior player LOL! The reality is quite different. It is not to denounce anyone who has achieved a WTA or ATP point because they are playing at an international level. We have the utmost respect for the level of play they have achieved. The two pro tours are punishing physically and mentally. Most important though is financially it will cripple you without support from benefactors, sponsors or federations. We still have friends who are 35 years of age who are living on people's couches and trying to play at the lower levels of the pro tour. The benefits are that they are fit and tanned, but they have limited prospects, often no spouse or kids. The clock is ticking, and they have hung on for too long. Think of it as a stock transaction when the market is going down, but for some reason, you hang on because of the delusion that you might be the last person standing. This is not to mean you shouldn't try. You absolutely should try to become a professional player if you have the skill and the will, but as we said earlier, all goals should be closely guarded by reflection. As high-performance coaches, we would be lying if we did not say some part of us would love to have any kid we teach be the next great pro. We certainly are fortunate to be part of the community of high-performance coaches looking to help develop our American players to that next level. However, our goal is to help players of all levels enjoy the journey.

We believe in options. When we graduated from high school, we had options. The same was true when we graduated from college and still today as coaches our competitive advantage is that we have options. Coaching is not a default or accidental profession for the two of us. Jeremy could still be on Capitol Hill where he worked for a US Senator and at the White House, and Tim could still be on Wall Street. Instead, we chose our pathway in tennis, and that is the point of this chapter. Choose your pathway, calling or passion. Don't do what your peers are doing. Do what you want to do and feel called to do!

Summary

You have one junior career in any chosen sport. Do it because you want to be the best you can be, and see through goal setting, reflection, and counsel where that will take you.

What College Tennis Coaches Are Looking for In a Prospect

David Redding

If you ask 100 college tennis coaches to list the top qualities they look for in a prospective student-athlete, you will most likely get 100 different answers, especially as to what they consider paramount. I do think, however, that just about every one of those lists would include the following:

1. **Strong Character** – displays high ethical standards of integrity, honesty, sportsmanship, and respect for others.
2. **Loves the Battle** – displays a passion for the game, a passion for the journey to be their best, and loves to compete!
3. **Physically Exceptional** – displays one or more of the following: good footwork, speed, quickness, good hands, strength, and finesse.
4. **Mentally Tough** – displays the ability to be comfortable with the uncomfortable and is unflappable regardless of the situation.
5. **Academically Sound** – displays good study habits, good grades, and solid ACT or SAT scores.
6. **Coachable** – demonstrates the ability not only to accept feedback, but seeks it out and acts on it.
7. **Strong Work Ethic** – displays the ability to push him/herself in practice or the classroom, and displays the will to prepare.
8. **Team Oriented** – displays the ability to celebrate teammates' successes and can support and encourage them when struggling.
9. **Self-Reliant** – displays the ability to initiate and proactively communicate with coaches and can complete tasks in the recruiting process without relying on Mom or Dad.

10. **Grit/Resilience** – displays the ability to keep going despite obstacles, and can adjust and bounce back after setbacks.
11. **Quiet Confidence** – displays the ability to balance a deep belief in his/her ability to get the job done with humility and lack of ego.
12. **Tennis IQ** – displays situational awareness on court. Understands momentum, and knows when to play the percentages and when to take risks.
13. **Skill Level Appropriate** – has done appropriate research on the UTR of the current players and is compatible with it.
14. **Grateful** – displays gratitude for opportunities, teachers, coaches, and mentors.
15. **Winning Habits** – is organized, punctual, and prepared!

David Redding Bio

David Redding, former Director of Tennis at Northwood Club in Dallas, Texas, is the Head Men's and Women's Tennis Coach at Harding University in Searcy, Arkansas. David was one of Jeremy's first tennis coaches. He is also a certified USPTA Elite Professional Coach.

The Positive Role of Social Media in the Junior Tennis Journey – Digital Tattoos, the Footrace, and the Reflection

Jenny Walls Robb

My brother has a variety of tattoos; some more meaningful than others. I've never asked, but I wonder if he regrets any of them. I don't have any tattoos—not because I think they are bad or offensive, but simply because I've never been able to decide on something to ink permanently on my body. Tattoos communicate aspects of an individual's identity—how we present ourselves and how other people perceive us. Social media is, in essence, a digital tattoo; and digital tattoos exist far longer than physical tattoos.

We construct technology, but technology also constructs us. Consider the evolution of text messaging. In the beginning, cell phones required users to scroll through the alphabet to select each letter to type a word. It was tedious and slow. Then smart keyboards came along—no more scrolling for letters. Then language changed to acronyms and emojis. Now you can choose the color of your emoji; your smiley face isn't simply yellow, you can choose from a spectrum of pale and dark to embody you.

Social media is a powerful medium offering a space to share your authentic voice and make real connections. However, it can also be a space of illusion and misconception. Freedom of speech does not equal freedom from consequences. If you put it out there, you own it—it's a reflection of who you are and what you believe. There are plenty of examples of what not to do. Chances are, if you think it might be inappropriate, it probably is. Let's focus instead on good practices. Posts should be positive, authentic, and rooted in reality. The same is true for your tennis journey.

1. **Say thank you.** Show gratitude to those who support you—your fans, teammates, family, coaches, trainers, and staff.
2. **Support others.** Share the successes of teammates or peers in other sports or programs and activities.
3. **Have fun.** Join in conversations and share interesting or humorous news.
4. **Engage with those you admire.** Social media offers a unique connection to people you may not otherwise have an opportunity to know.
5. **Be present.** Experience with all your senses what is happening in the present moment—in other words, see, hear, smell, taste, and feel. Avoid the state of "constantly doing" and make time for "simply being."

According to Greek mythology, Atalanta's father wanted her to marry, but she agreed to marry only if her suitors could outrun her in a footrace. Those who lost were killed. Many young men died in pursuit of Atalanta. Hippomenes asked the goddess Aphrodite for help, and she gave him three golden apples. The apples were irresistible, so each time Atalanta was ahead of Hippomenes, he rolled an apple ahead of her. She would be distracted and chase after it instead, allowing Hippomenes to win the footrace. Regarding social media, we should caution against chasing after distractions.

Another cautionary tale from Greek mythology is that of Narcissus. He was very beautiful, and many fell in love with him, but he only showed his admirers condescension and disrespect. While Narcissus was hunting, the nymph Echo saw him and immediately fell in love. When she revealed her love to him, he rejected her. In despair, she roamed the woods for the rest of her life until all that was left of her was an echo. Nemesis, the goddess of revenge, led Narcissus to a pool. Upon seeing his reflection for the first time, he immediately fell in love, which led to his despair and eventual death. This serves as a warning against self-absorption, vanity, and egotism.

Social media offers a variety of platforms through which you can share your experiences, thoughts, and opinions; and connect with others—it is social after all. In the words of Bill S. Preston, Esq., "Be excellent to each other."

<u>Jenny Walls Robb Bio</u>
Jenny grew up playing a variety of youth sports in Birmingham, Alabama before playing NCAA Division I tennis at Samford University where she earned her Bachelor of Arts in English/Language Arts. Jenny is passionate about education. She is an Elite Professional in the USPTA and earned the distinction of Master of Tennis - Junior Development, in addition to a Professional Certification in Adult Development with the PTR. Jenny is a Master Tennis Performance Specialist with the ITPA and a faculty member of the United States Tennis Congress. Jenny's goal as a coach is to develop healthy, injury-free athletes of good character with a solid foundation of fundamental techniques and tactics while nurturing a life-long love of the sport. Her goal as Director of Marketing & Communications for USTA Alabama is to promote and grow the game. As USPTA-Alabama President, she hopes to raise the standards of tennis-teaching professionals and coaches.

Nutrition for Junior Tennis Players: The Importance of Fueling-Up

> "The doctor of the future will give no medicine but will interest his patients in the care of the human frame, in diet and in the cause and prevention of disease."
> **Thomas Edison**
>
> "Let food be your medicine."
> **Hippocrates**

Dr. Charlotte Alabaster

The importance of proper nutrition for healthy growth, development, and optimal performance is widely accepted amongst medical professionals, coaches, and parents. **In the following chapter, coaches, parents and athletes will find performance enhancing information through the power of good nutrition.**

Overview of proper nutrition for children and teens

The nutritional requirements of any child or teen will vary with age and stage of growth. A child's food preferences, food allergies, and intolerances are just three of the factors parents face when attempting to meet the dietary demands of their young athletes. Creating a well-balanced diet that includes all the food groups and micronutrients can be a bit like finding the Holy Grail. It's not easy being a tennis parent in today's world. In many families, both parents work, so finding time for meal preparation can be tough. In other families, children are being raised by a single parent, which can create additional time constraints. Much time is often spent driving to coaching sessions within the home city and traveling to tournaments out of town. In this chapter parents and coaches will find practical ways of feeding their young players a healthy diet both at home and when traveling.

Nutrition for Little Ones - ages 3-6

Small children have small stomachs, and their physiology is more delicate than that of an adult. They are more vulnerable to the ill effects of heat, and although this chapter is on nutrition, it would be an oversight to neglect the importance of hydration in all children, especially the very young. Frequent bathroom breaks to urinate are reassuring and show that fluid intake is adequate. Dizziness, fainting, or decreased urine output with dark urine is indicative of dehydration and can pose a serious threat to well-being.

Snacks and meals throughout the day are needed to fill the small stomachs of this age group. Easy to digest foods are favored:
- Bananas
- Avocados
- Hummus with celery sticks
- Cucumber
- Meat stews
- Bolognaise
- Whole grain noodles
- Cheese sauce made with whole grain flour
- Brown rice
- Oatmeal
- Applesauce
- Smoked salmon
- Nuts if tolerated (almonds, peanuts, walnuts)
- Raisins
- Baked beans
- Toast
- Cheese (goat cheese is easier to digest than cheese from cow's milk)

Pre-pubertal children and pubescent teens need a lot of calories and foods rich in vitamins, micronutrients, and minerals to provide the building blocks to develop a strong, healthy body that reaches its full growth potential. Adequate sleep is also vital for growth. While this is not addressed in detail in this chapter, it is part of the energy balance.

The most important meal of the day is still breakfast, and a warm breakfast is recommended rather than a smoothie. The reason for this is that the process of chewing (mastication) adds saliva to the food and exercises the jaw which is an essential energetic activity that enhances the digestive process. Leftover stews, or dinner from the previous evening, can make an excellent breakfast. Many folks eat cereals, but these foods are often highly processed, and although many micronutrients are listed, they are often present in inadequate amounts. Oatmeal is a good option especially if nuts and raisins are added. Whole-meal toast with baked beans is an easy, nutritious breakfast, too. Cheese on toast, sardines on toast, tuna sandwich, or avocados and hummus can also make a healthy nutritious meal and are quick to prepare.

I would also encourage parents to provide warm drinks for their kids in the mornings. Loading the stomach with cold milk out of the fridge is convenient but not the best way to make energy cycle first thing in the morning. Lemon water, tea, coffee, or non-coffee substitutes are all viable options for warm drinks at the start of the day and can be consumed on the way to school or practice if time is limited. Sometimes appetites are not the best in the mornings especially if kids are short on sleep. So, getting to bed in good time is important but can be difficult when there are school projects to complete and other extracurricular activities to fit in.

According to Canada's Food Guide, there are four main food groups: fruits and vegetables, grain products, dairy and alternatives, and meat and alternatives. This is by no means the definitive last word on how a diet should look but is a useful point of reference.

Getting sufficient calories on board is always tricky for kids going through a growth spurt and who are also very active. It is reassuring when a child is eating well and sleeping soundly, even if they are on the lean side. Foods that are high in calories, micronutrients/minerals, and vitamins are whole grains (including wheat and rice), pulses (including lentils and split peas) and beans, and nuts of all kinds. Dairy is an important source of calories and vitamins such as A and D, calcium, magnesium, and phosphorus, but this is not the only food group that supplies these nutrients. It is so important to have a variety of foods to provide a range of nutrients and micronutrients.

There is synergy between various foods with enhanced absorption which is why eating a wide variety of foods is so important. Vitamin D, for example, may work with hepcidin during the process of iron absorption, a vitamin we usually associate with calcium metabolism. Eating a little bit of everything and not too much of anything is a great way to ensure a healthy, balanced diet.

Some kids do not like certain fruits or vegetables. If there are fruits and vegetables that they do like, encourage them to eat these and make sure they are readily available. It is not worth getting into a power struggle about eating things that the palate does not enjoy. Pick your battles - this one is not worth the fighting.

Meats and fish are an essential source of protein, B12, zinc (B13), and iron.

If there were only two micronutrients to emphasize as important for athletes, they would be Vitamin D and iron. All are important in different ways to health and well-being, but without adequate Vitamin D children run the risk of developing rickets and not forming healthy bones and teeth. Also, Vitamin D improves muscle function and balance which are both very important for a tennis player of any age. Vitamin D3 is converted in the kidneys from Vitamin D2 in the skin after exposure to sunshine. One might assume that sun exposure would be sufficient, but above latitude 37 degrees N (Colorado City and Cairo) and below 37 degrees S (Auckland and Buenos Aires Province in Argentina) the sunlight is not striking the skin at the right angle even in the summer to produce sufficient amounts of D2. To be sure your athletes are getting enough Vitamin D3, supplements on a daily basis are recommended: 1200 iu for children of less than 50 kgs (or 110 pounds) and 2000 iu daily for children weighing more than 50 kgs.

In addition, sunblock prevents the sun from doing its usual work with Vitamin D2 production, so even in sunny climates, it is advisable to take vitamin D3 to ensure adequate amounts are available for bone health and growth. The cost of Vitamin D supplements is around 10 dollars for a bottle of 90 tabs. If tablets cannot be swallowed, Vitamin D3 is also available as a liquid. It is noteworthy that although Vitamin D3 is called a vitamin, it functions as a hormone in the body governing bone metabolism. To achieve optimal absorption of Vitamin D3, vitamin K2 is required which is found in milk from grass-fed cows, in eggs from grass-fed chickens, and is produced in the healthy human gut. Antibiotics, however, can impair the ability of the gut to synthesize its own K2. Some vitamin D3 supplements are combined with K2. In children, carbonated drinks should be avoided because they interfere with the process of making strong, healthy bones.

Children who experience leg cramps at night may be deficient in vitamin D, and if they are not already taking supplements, it would be wise to start. If the leg cramps improve, it is very likely that the child was vitamin D deficient, but check with your pediatrician or family physician to be certain.

Iron is another vital micronutrient. The biggest problem with iron is that it is not readily absorbed. On any given day only 10% of the intake is absorbed from the gut. Exercise, especially in an explosive sport like tennis, consumes iron through on-court activity. During growth, additional iron requirements are needed, and boys can become deficient at puberty with associated loss of form and fatigue.

In girls, the issue is even more serious. If during the prepubertal years there are inadequate iron stores from poor eating habits, there will be problems with iron deficiency with the onset of menstruation. If the cycles are regular with heavy blood loss, the girl will be fatigued, lack stamina and strength on the court, and show an inevitable decline in performance. With thoughtfulness to nutrition in the prepubescent years (and this is variable as some girls will start menstruation at around 9, although 13 would be more usual) this iron deficient state can often be avoided. Foods that are rich in iron are red meat, beef, lamb, venison, bison, wild meat and game, and salmon. The haem iron found in meat is far more readily absorbed than non-haem iron derived from plant sources. This is very important to know because some teens may be vegetarian, and this adds yet another barrier to getting enough iron and increases the risk of iron deficiency and anemia. Other sources of iron are eggs, lentils, chickpeas, hummus, black beans, baked beans, sardines, and leafy greens. Nuts are also often iron-rich. Almonds, walnuts, pumpkin seeds, and raisins are also a good source of iron.

In general eating meat with vegetables and fruit enhances the absorption of iron. Hepcidin is a hormone that may rise with exercise, and it can interfere with the absorption of iron. This is another reason to ensure that young athletes get enough rest and time to recover.

Dairy and grains such as oatmeal and cereals inhibit the absorption of iron while citrus fruits such as oranges and grapefruits rich in vitamin C enhance absorption. If a child has become iron deficient with a ferritin of less than 50 and showing a decline in performance, iron supplementation is indicated under the supervision of a medical professional, family doctor, or pediatrician. It will take at least six months in a menstruating teenager to get these levels back to normal using oral supplements. In severe iron deficiency with anemia, iron infusions may be used to restore levels more rapidly. It is important to remember that iron-fortified cereals are a poor source of iron. The quantities per 100 grams are minimal. Eating the cereal with milk decreases the absorption. Reading the small print on food labels is essential.

Children who are iron deficient will experience a decline in performance with less endurance and stamina and increased infections, colds, and sore throats. Fatigue with increased sleep requirements, irritability, tearfulness, shortness of breath, and palpitations are also symptoms that occur commonly in iron deficiency.

If a child is iron deficient, medical supervision is needed with additional iron either as an oral supplement or, if severe, as an infusion. Levels may be monitored with blood work. The target level is ferritin of 50 or more. Once deficiency occurs, it can take six months to restore the levels to normal, longer if menstrual losses are excessive. Also, the intensity and frequency of training will need to be adjusted during this recovery phase. As iron levels rise and performance improves, training frequency and intensity may be gradually increased.

It is important for coaches to realize that obese kids may be malnourished. They may be eating insufficient calories, and the basal metabolic rate will have slowed, too. This is very unhealthy but not uncommon.

Special Diets

It is also not uncommon for children to be lactose intolerant, gluten sensitive, or have other food sensitivities. It is possible with some effort to provide adequate calories and micronutrients. It can, however, be a challenge.

Diarrhea in athletes

It is not uncommon for athletes to experience exercise-induced diarrhea. Happy Bars, a low-FODMAP energy bar, are specially formulated to avoid making this problem worse.

Eating for tournaments

Coaches and parents can do their players and kids a great favor by packing a supply of various dry foods to take on the trip. Examples include oatmeal for a warm breakfast, adding nuts and raisins for additional nutrients, and nut bars. If staying for a while at a tournament, Google the nearest supermarkets and buy bananas, apples, and avocados, all of which make for healthy snacks. Also, pack tea bags so that all you need is hot water to make a warm drink.

Tournament sites often provide burgers at lunchtime. It is good for the athlete to have access to a variety of foods, and parents and coaches can help a great deal to ensure this happens. Post-match, it is advisable to eat within 45 minutes of play. A combination of protein and complex carbohydrates is ideal to hasten recovery.

If the player does not have much of an appetite after the match, a warm drink is better than nothing with a snack of their choice but avoid sugary foods if possible.

As an interesting piece of diet trivia and a benchmark for the kind of calorie intake needed at an elite level, Michael Phelps eats 12,000 calories per day but not nearly enough fruits and vegetables to satisfy his nutrient requirements.

Quinoa can cause abdominal cramps in some people, so if this is part of the diet, try excluding it and see if symptoms improve.

Courtside snacks can be game savers, and the easiest go-to snacks are bananas and happy bars. It is a shame to lose a match from hunger, but I have seen it happen to juniors.

Food is medicine, and providing a nutritious diet is essential for good health, consistent maximal performance, and reaching the full growth potential.

Resources: *Eat, Fit, Play* by Jeff Rothschild, Authority Nutrition, Canada Food Guide, *Beat the Iron Crisis* by Leonard Mervyn

Dr. Charlotte Alabaster Bio

Charlotte hails from the UK where she graduated in medicine, from the University of London, England in 1982. She now resides in Calgary, Alberta, Canada where she works in fulltime family practice. Passionate about tennis since she was a preschooler, she is actively engaged in the tennis coaching community sharing pearls of medical knowledge acquired over a lifetime of practice.

Point 3
Elite Training for All Levels

Essential Qualities of Good Training

"People who write about spring training not being necessary have never tried to throw a ball."
Sandy Koufax

"I don't really think about the degree of difficulty or the possibility of making a mistake. I just try to relax and let my preparation and training take over."
Simone Biles

By way of introduction, we want to mention that writing this book relates to training. Before we wrote our first book, we had only written articles and given presentations at conferences. Then one day we realized that those articles and presentations had served as training and preparation for authoring a whole book. In the same way, compared to our first book which took three years to create from inception to publication, this second book took eight months to complete. Writing the first book was like training for writing another one. In the process, we learned how to be more efficient at what we were doing as writers just as players can learn to be more efficient with how they train on the court. We certainly never planned on being authors but found it to be a rewarding way to continue learning about the game and sharing what we had learned with others.

The essential qualities of training for a player at any level should **provide the technical, tactical, physical, and mental components to help the athlete perform at his/her very best level.** These qualities give the player the best chance to improve long-term. Regardless of a player's level, coaches should have this as their top goal with every player they mentor. Coaches should be both *productive* and *purposeful* as they work with their players toward this lifelong goal. There are certain guidelines the best coaches follow as they prepare their players for elite training.

The very best coaches demonstrate these characteristics:

Engaging – This means that training and practices are engaging for both the coach and the players. If it is only engaging for one of the two, then the chance of learning new skills will be severely decreased.

Long term focused – Any tips, strategies, suggestions and other comments by coaches should be solely focused on what will help the student in the long term, not just short term.

Focused on Constant Improvement – This sounds obvious, but the reality is whatever goals a player has and whatever they are doing should revolve around specific improvement toward those goals, not just busy work that keeps them occupied during the lesson or class.

Time-Oriented - One of the skills coaches are paid for is time management. As we have grown as coaches, we have come to respect this concept and gotten better at it over time. What do we mean by this? Whether you are teaching a 10 and under red ball class, a beginner high school level class or elite high-performance players, one of the barometers of a good lesson is how well a coach manages the time. Through our continuing education, we have learned a specific formula for percentages of time regarding athletic warmup, skill development, game development and cool down.

Efficient – Any practice or lesson must be efficient. This means establishing the goal of the lesson and doing activities that are directed toward achieving that goal. While good coaches have knowledge, great coaches only share the knowledge that is needed at that time.

The amount of time and dedication that successful junior players put into their training is more than typical youngsters would sacrifice. The key is to be the best you can be. As players, you should train to be your best and, through guidance and experience, develop parameters for your training that put you in the most productive environment.

So what are the best components of training for a junior player that garner maximum results? They are as follows:

Technical, Tactical, Physical, Mental, Emotional and Match Play. No one component is more important than another but together, if firing on the same productive cylinders, will allow the aspiring player one day to become *the complete junior tennis player*. As we learned from our high-performance training, a coach should follow these principles when training a student – **patience, progressions, parameters, planning, and problem-solving.**

Since we analyze the physical, mental and emotional aspects of player development in more detail in other parts of the book, we will briefly examine technical, tactical, physical and match play training in this chapter.

Technical – Technical training must start with knowing which **skill, shot and situation** you are practicing. You could call this the S's of technical analysis. This means that you practice more than just the volley for example but specifically practice which volley—low, high, or medium. Also, be aware of the situation in which you are hitting the volley in—offense, defense or neutral. Here's a good pattern for training: (a) the coach analyzes the shot in a live ball situation with no tips given, (b) the coach defines the primary issue with the shot, (c) the coach trains the player using a corrective technique in a closed coach-feeding situation with a defined purpose for where the player is hitting the shot, (d) the player practices the new skill in a competitive situation and then (e) finally puts the shot to work in actual match play. The biggest mistake we see with training is when a coach evaluates a shot in a closed situation with the player hearing the tips from the coach before the coach observes how the player hits the shot in live ball play. It might be frustrating for you to be missing the shot to start off, but this is the best way a coach can mentor you as a player and identify how to improve your shot-making. The best coaches will help you focus on which part of the stroke you are practicing – **stance, footwork, backswing, contact point, forward swing or follow through.**

Equally important when training is practicing the various stages of receiving the ball and anticipating how and where the ball is coming. This can be done in simple ways such as calling out (by the time the ball gets to the net) such characteristics of your opponent's shot as ball depth (deep or short), ball spin (flat, topspin or slice) or ball speed (fast or slow). This can be done in a "coach fed" environment or cooperative live ball play. You can also break down anticipating the ball into these two areas; reading how the ball is coming and reacting accordingly with your movement. We will discuss footwork in more detail in a later chapter. Ensuring this is part of your training as a player helps with how to recognize, decide and move to the ball. We will discuss later footwork patterns and other components that correlate to ball depth, spin, and speed.

Tactical – Here you need to understand three main things—**the geometry of the court, your strengths, and your weakness.** It's best to train in this order. Geometry of the court must come first because it dictates why you move, how you move and where you move. Remember, you recover off center when hitting crosscourt because of the possible angles of your opponent's response. Once you understand the geometry of the court, you can focus next on how to use your strengths. It's just as important to practice your strengths as well as address your weaknesses. We have been guilty ourselves of focusing too much on players' weaknesses. Proper training involves constantly strengthening your strengths while at the same time minimizing your weaknesses.

Physical – The physical components of training as defined by the USPTA include **motor skills, conditioning, speed, agility and quickness, strength, nutrition, flexibility and medical.** All of these are important. Instead of covering all these components here, they have been examined in other chapters including insight by guest industry experts.

Match Play – Before jumping into full match play put stipulations on competitive match play. For example, practice second serves by playing tie-breaks with only one serve, hitting your second serve returns down the line and coming into net, or mixing up your game by hitting topspin and slice shots from the baseline. Then go into all full match play. When going into full match play be aware of which ways you want to win points – **force errors from your opponent with the direction of your shot, depth of your shot, the spin of your shot, or speed of your shot.** Also, be aware of what type of playing style you want to bring to the match – **serve and volley, counterpuncher, or aggressive baseliner.** All these styles have produced world class players, many of which end up as No. 1, so identify which one works best for you in match play and go with it!

Summary

We hope this chapter has helped you better discern how to make your training and practices productive and purposeful and not just busy work.

Power of Percentages – Singles and Doubles

"You will always miss 100% of the shots you don't take."
Wayne Gretzky

"Things get done only if the data we gather can inform and inspire those in a position to make a difference."
Mike Schmoker, Author of *Results*

In this chapter, our goal is to demonstrate the ways you can use data to create "best training practices" for both singles and doubles. First, let's look at a typical scenario for a player. It's 4-4 in the first set, and you have your first break point in a 2 out of 3 set match, and your opponent hits you a sitter second serve right in your wheelhouse, and you crank your forehand service return into the back fence. This is a situation all players from the club level to the pros need to know how to handle. What do you do? Do you get upset or move on? How do you handle the mistake? If you get upset, where is the pressure coming from that makes you mad? Are you suddenly remembering too late how your coach trained you to hit this shot? These are all important questions that a player should be aware of, and we will discuss them in this chapter.

Singles

The good news is missing this return is not the end of the world when you play percentage tennis. Before we examine some relevant statistics about the return of serve, let's look at some basic percentages of five phases of play in tennis. Tennis, as mentioned in the introduction, is based on five phases – serve, return of serve, baseline play, attacking the net and opponent attacking the net. This means that each phase takes up 20% of the game. So, if you are practicing baseline play, you are only practicing 20% of the game and ignoring the other 80%. While there are certainly times in practice where you should be focusing on one phase of the game, be careful about doing that for too long. Even Rafael Nadal is good at volleys. This would be like golfers only practicing their drive and not working on their putting or short game, or pitchers in baseball just practicing the fastball.

In this chapter, we will address how to use the data we know about percentage tennis to make you the best singles player possible. We first look at data and then apply it to your game. Many of these statistics come from Craig O'Shannessey's brain game site and the ATP and WTA player statistics portions of their websites. We will also take the same approach for doubles after reviewing singles.

Singles – Return of Serve

Let's go back to return of serve. Roger Federer's career break points converted is 41%. This means that Roger has converted less than half of his break point chances during match play throughout his career. This statistic comes from the ATP statistics part of their website as of 3/18/2018. Why is this important? It's important because tennis is not a game of perfection or absolutes. Even a player as great as Federer still wins most of his matches regardless of how many break points he converts.

Let's compare tennis to other sports. In almost all other sport, the winner must win more points to be the winner. In many Olympic sports, for example, the focus might be on scoring a perfect 10. However, in tennis, these goals help, but they are not the overriding reasons why someone wins a match. Winning in tennis boils down to winning the right points at the right time. For example, if you are playing a 2 out of 3 three sets match, you could lose the first set 6-0 and then win the next two sets each in tie-break to win the overall match. So, losing a one-sided first set then closely winning the next two sets means it is possible to lose more points than your opponent but still win the match. To be exact, in the scenario just described, you could lose 72 points, and the opponent could lose 62 points, and you would still win the match.

You can play the **worst tennis of your life and the best tennis of your life all in one match and end up as the champion.**

Singles – Total Points Won in Match

"Let's look at some further statistics. If you win 55% percent of your points in a match, research has shown a high correlation to winning. For example, from 1991-2016 the average amount of points won in a season for a No. 1 player in the world was just 55%" (Craig O'Shannessey, braingametennis.com, *the Most Important Number in Tennis)*. "In 2016 Andy Murray (No. 1 that year) won 90% of matches and only won 55% of his points." (Craig O'Shannessey, brain gametennis.com, *The Most Important Number in Tennis)*. Furthermore, Roger Federer's, Rafael Nadal's and Novak Djokovic's total points won in their careers are each 54% (ATP statistics page as of 3/18/2018). Pretty amazing how they are the same!

Singles - Serve

Now let's look at serve numbers. First serve percentage for Roger Federer is 62% and for Rafael Nadal it is 69%. Roger Federer's, Rafael Nadal's, and Serena Williams's *first serve points won* career percentages are 77%, 72%, and 74%, respectively. Roger Federer's, Rafael Nadal's, and Serena William's *second serve points won* career percentages are 57%, 57%, and 58%, respectively (ATP/WTA statistics 3/18/2018).

Singles – Winners vs. Errors

What about winners versus errors? In the 2015 Australian Open the stats show the following - men = 70% errors vs. 30% winners and women = 74% errors vs. 26% winners (Craig O'Shannessey, brain gametennis.com). These stats tell us that even the world's best sometimes make more mistakes than winners.

Singles – Length of Rally

Another crucial aspect of understanding tennis percentages is knowing the average rally length of our sport. The statistics point to the importance of the 4-shot rally length (Craig O'Shannessey, braingametennis.com). The consistent data shows that 70% percent of rallies at the pro level are 0-4 shots, which includes serve+1 & return+1 (Craig O'Shannessey, braingametennis.com). Even at the highest level of juniors, this trend applies. The International Tennis Federation (ITF) players perform 4.4 to 4.8 shots in one point. Boys' points on average last 10 seconds and girls 12 seconds (https://www.armbeep.com/many-shots-junior-tennis-players-hit-per-week/).

Not only is our game dominated by the first four shots, but the best players win more points in this range. For example, in the 2015 Australian Open, 69% of all points Novak Djokovic played were zero to four; 21% were in the five to eight range, and only 10% were in the range of nine or more shots (stats that come from https://www.theguardian.com/sport/2016/jun/24/what-makes-novak-djokovic-perfect-tennis-player-hard-to-beat-wimbledon).

The following statistics shows a similar trend on clay from the 2016 French Open Final between Andy Murray and Novak Djokovic (Craig O'Shannessey, braingametennis.com).

2016 French Open Final Rally Lengths

	0-4 Shot Rallies Won	**5-8 Shot Rallies Won**	**9+ Shot Rallies Won**
Set 1	Djokovic: 10, Murray: 15	Djokovic: 6, Murray: 9	Djokovic: 8, Murray: 8
Set 2	Djokovic: 16, Murray: 9	Djokovic: 6, Murray: 3	Djokovic: 7, Murray: 3
Set 3	Djokovic: 19, Murray: 17	Djokovic: 8, Murray: 2	Djokovic: 6, Murray: 6
Set 4	Djokovic: 17, Murray, 11	Djokovic: 12, Murray: 6	Djokovic: 7, Murray: 8
Total	**Djokovic: 62, Murray: 52**	**Djokovic: 32, Murray: 20**	**Djokovic: 28, Murray: 25**

Singles – Net Game

Finally, it is important to look at the net game percentages. While perfection is difficult to achieve it is not necessary for winning. Let's look at Rafael Nadal. In the 2017 U.S. Open Final against Kevin Anderson, Nadal won 100% of his net points, 16 for 16 at the net. While this is certainly impressive, it is not the norm for most pro players. Over Nadal's career, the percentage of points he won at the net is 81% (https://www.tennisprofiler.com/nadal). We will look later in this chapter at the main things Rafa does to be successful at the net. First, let's look at some other key players. Roger Federer's, Simona Halep's, Lleyton Hewitt's and Andre Agassi's percentage of points won at the net over their careers are 73%, 71%, 72% and 76%, respectively. (https://www.tennisprofiler.com/federer, https://www.tennisprofiler.com/halep). The average of these five players (including Nadal) is 75%. While these numbers seem pretty good, again they are not perfect.

Summarize Data

As you can see from these statistics, no players are perfect. This is the beauty of tennis. A player's success is not based on perfection and never will be. Now that we know what the data tell us, let's apply it to how players should train and play.

First, we need to summarize what all this data means. Players at all levels need to put any mistakes, unforced errors or missed opportunities in proper perspective. For example, how many times in singles do players get lobbed and lose the point because they came into the net? Unfortunately, because of this one point, they may decide now not to attack the net. The reality is when a player attacks the net the geometry of angles available on the court for put away shots is in the net player's favor. What if Stefan Edberg, Patrick Rafter, John McEnroe, or Pete Sampras just stopped coming to the net after being lobbed couple of times? They would not be using the proper perspective or utilizing their strengths as a player to become as successful as they were.

Let's go back to an example at the beginning where you miss an easy second serve return on break point chance. If you are aware that Roger Federer converts less than half of his break points, then you have a better chance of relaxing a little after making such an error instead of getting frustrated because you understand percentage tennis.

Knowing percentage tennis means understanding patterns in each area of play – **serve, return of serve, baseline play, and net play** - and using games in practice that will simulate match play. We will discuss some of the games that have been most effective for practicing these areas that any junior player could do using appropriate equipment and court size, based on age and level.

Singles – Serve and Serve + 1

The serve at any level of play should be practiced with purpose and placement. For example, purpose means knowing if you are hitting a second serve with kick and placement means knowing what zone of the service box you are hitting to – wide, middle, or T. One of the main reasons why Roger Federer, Rafael Nadal, and Serena Williams and other world class players are successful is their ability to place their serves to set up their weapons on the next shot.

One of the biggest barriers to continuing with tennis, once players start, involves getting frustrated while learning to serve. If serve practice is not included in lessons, then the overall development of the player's game will be greatly limited. Let's face it. You must be able to serve well to win tennis matches. While tennis coaches know the importance of the serve, coaching it can be a challenge as we know and therefore can sometimes be put on the back burner in practice.

While players sometimes want to just "get the serve in the box," this philosophy does not match with the realities of our sport. One game to make serve placement more fun for players is one called *"Heat Seeker."* This is a game to help players focus on the placement of their serves. Players start by hitting a certain number of serves in the service box. Next, the service box is divided into half and players hit into both halves a certain amount of times. Finally, divide the service box into thirds, and the players must hit into each third a certain number of times. This game can be applied based on the players' level and ability.

As previously mentioned, our sport is dominated by shorter rallies in both the men's and women's game. Through our USTA High Performance continuing education training we have learned the importance of serve + 1 strategies. Since emphasizing games with serve + 1 practice, we have found players to be more focused and enjoy practicing the strategy and technique of placing the serve. Once we included more games with the serve practice, we heard comments such as "this is fun" or "can I keep hitting to this target in the box?"

Here are some examples of how practice games related to the serve work. *"Around the World Wipeout"* was a serve placement game that our players helped us create. We started out playing the game having two sections in the service box or three sections (wide, middle, T) for players to aim for. Once players hit a certain number of serves into that section, they move on to the next one. The first person to hit each section the established number of times wins. One day as we were playing this game, one of the kids said, "Why don't we set up a pyramid of balls in each section and if you knock the pyramid over you get to move onto the next session automatically." We said, "Sounds great!" With the added challenge of knocking over the pyramids, the players felt more ownership of what they are doing and had more fun.

A tweak we added to this serve game just mentioned is to have two teams playing each other with two players on each team. They follow the same rules as before. However, we add movement after the serve. We have one player serve, and one player is waiting to hand toss (in a safe spot) after the serve. After the serving player does his/her serve, the other player on the team from a safe distance hand tosses a ball for the serving player on his/her team to hit to the open court. Once this is done twice the two switch roles. The team that successfully does serve and serve +1 a certain number of times wins. We found this was a great way to ensure players are practicing footwork after their serves and ensure everyone is involved and keeps moving.

Singles - Return of Serve

Let's look at some specific statistics for Rafael Nadal. Rafa is number one and third career-wise on the ATP tour statistics page for return of serve (5/19/2018). His *1st Serve Return Points Won Percentage* is 35.4%, and his *2nd Serve Return Points Won Percentage* is 57.6% (5/19/2018).

One game we use is called "*Rafa Return.*" It is based on Rafa's second serve return winning percentage. One player serves ten points only hitting second serves. The other player is looking to hit attacking returns and win 6 out of 10 of the points. Each player does this once.

Singles – Combining Serve and Return of Serve

Another game we like to do is called "*The Four Shot Challenge.*" This is a game that emphasizes the importance of serve +1 and return + 1. This can be done with any level. There are two teams with a group of four players. The teams are competing to see who can make the first four shots (serve, return, serve + 1, return +1) cooperatively. Each time they get all four shots, it counts as a point. You can see which team gets to a certain number of points first. If players have trouble doing this cooperative drill, then they can change the distance from the net from which they are serving, the type of ball used or the action the players are performing (maybe a throw instead of a serve).

A game we like to do for serve and return of serve is called "*All In.*" This game helps players have the confidence to go after their serve or return of serve during pressure situations like a tie-break. Two players play a 12 tie-break, first to seven points by two. If players get to 6-6, the next point wins. One player serves the whole time with the other player returning the entire time. Then they play again with the other player serving.

Singles - Baseline Play

We have learned through our years of coaching that consistency is great, but consistency with no purpose is of little value to a player's training. Lets' take the goal of two players hitting 100 balls back and forth in a row. Sure, the worlds' best could easily do this, but do they do that in a match? The previous stats tell us no. Through our continuing education, we have been fortunate enough to learn from many great minds on this topic. We want to share some best practices when it comes to training baseline play.

Let's relate this to playing an instrument such as the piano. For anyone who took piano lessons, you know you don't start playing Mozart's Symphony N. 40 when you first touch the piano keys unless you are a piano prodigy. You practice scales with one hand then scales with the other and progress continually to harder piano skills. This means as a player you need to make sure you are getting the foundation of moving first without the racquet before you practice a Pete Sampras screamer forehand down the line. As players, we need to remember how vital the athleticism is to how you move. Roger Federer and Jack Sock have different forehands style-wise, but they move incredibly well. With that in mind, it is important to start any practice of a new stroke with a clear understanding of how to move for receiving the ball, hitting the ball and recovering for the next ball. One of the biggest reasons Roger reached No. 1 in the ATP rankings at age 36 (the oldest to be at this number in history) is his efficient movement. This is one reason people might say he is like a gazelle on the court, which we will discuss in more detail later.

A great way to start team practice with purpose and "focused consistency" is to start with training **these three primary ball controls - height, depth, and direction.** Have your players pair up and start by seeing how many balls they can hit in a row "scoreboard height" or higher. This means put tennis tape the height of where scorecards are or would be and see how many they can hit at or above the tape in a row. Then have pairs of players all rally for a certain depth as many times as they can in a row. Finally, have pairs hit crosscourt on the deuce and ad side for as many shots as they can in a row. Each drill should go for two minutes. At the end, have each pair add up its number from each drill. This is the pair's "ball control number." Players with similar "ball control numbers" can be placed together when doing drills or games during the practice.

Singles - Net Play

As we mentioned earlier, Rafael Nadal won 100% of his net points at the 2017 US Open. Over his career, he has won 81% of his net points. You might be saying how is he doing it? After all, he is not known for having stellar volley technique like Stefan Edberg, Pete Sampras or Patrick Rafter. However, he picks right times to come to net. What Rafael Nadal does so well is everything before he even hits the first volley. It's partly based on three factors - his balance when hitting the approach shot, his excellent decision making, and the placement of his approach shot. When working on net play, it is vital that you practice those three areas. We like to do a drill called *"Rafa Attack Drill."* Two players are hitting crosscourt for depth. Once they get a ball in their "wheelhouse," on balance and shortly behind the service line, they hit the ball into the open court, which is down the line, and come in for a volley. The two players play to ten.

Doubles

Now that we have analyzed singles, we will evaluate how to use percentage tennis in doubles. While the statistics are not as available for doubles, we can use some to establish certain games and training we believe to be helpful. For a more in-depth doubles strategy, there are numerous books out there on the subject. We will apply some best practices for doubles using the data that is available.

Doubles – Positioning/Formations

Let's first look at doubles based on the way the game is played. We need to understand that out of the three most commonly known formations in doubles, **one up and one back, both up and both back,** which one is the most effective. From our continuing education, we know that statistically the **most effective strategy for doubles success is both up and second is both back.** Why is this case? Because of what we like to call the power of the "invisible tether" between the two players ensuring that the movement of doubles is always considered team movement. So, when training for doubles make sure you practice drills that work on shifting together when you and your partner are at the net. We agree that a good rule of thumb is if one player's right foot is close to the singles line then his/her partner's right foot should be close to the center line. Imagine a tether forcing players to move together if one player shifts more to one side. This helps ensure that the team can cover the middle.

Doubles – Serve

Next, we examine serve doubles statistics and how we can properly train that part of the game. Look at what the statistics say about the serve in doubles. In Mark Hodgkinson's article on tennis player.net titled, "The Bryan Brothers: Principles of Winning Doubles" he says the following: "In singles, you can serve 50 percent and be fine, but in doubles, you need to serve in the high 70's." (Excerpt from his book, *Game, Set and Match*). Knowing this information, how can you train it effectively? All coaches have different approaches to this sort of training. It can be as simple as two teams playing tie-breaks by only hitting second serves to focus on higher percentage first serves.

Doubles – Return of Serve and Serve + 1

Now let's tackle return of serve. For most players, the strategy is crosscourt return in doubles. There are undoubtedly several advantages to that approach. You're hitting away from the net person, hitting a longer distance as compared to down the line and you have more time to get ready for the next shot. Whatever you do in doubles, make your returns as much as you can. Research has shown by making 80% of your returns you are applying enough pressure on the serving team to give yourself a chance to win. So, you could train this by playing doubles first to ten points in this way. One team serves the whole time alternating with a partner after every two serves. Your coach tracks as a team if you can get to 8 out of 10 of your returns in play. This can be called your team's return percentage.

We also need to be aware of the first shot after the serve, whether it be a volley or an approaching groundstroke. This does not have to be a volley. Whatever it is, make sure you are practicing that also.

Summary

While all coaches have their style for doing drills, we strive each day to ensure that whatever drills we do are based on data, facts, and systems that correctly reflect a winning game. If you want to play a sport to perfection, then tennis can be your sport, but the good news is you don't have to perfect to be good at it!

Using Video Analysis Technology Wisely

"Technology is just the tool. In terms of getting the kids working together and motivating them, the teacher is the most important."
Bill Gates

How do you use technology to help your tennis game? Jeremy remembers as a young junior in Texas utilizing camcorder technology to video tournaments or practice matches and watching them at home, and how useful that was to his game. With today's technology of video analysis on iPads and other devices, many players are taking advantage of it. We certainly recommend this and use a lot of video recording with our players. However, we have found that it must be used wisely and effectively to help players improve. In this chapter, we will discuss our thoughts on this topic.

First, players must understand why they are using video recording. Are you using it to analyze something during practice or matches? Are you using it to know how you are doing technically or tactically? Are you using it for doubles or singles? So, before you spend the money, time and effort to start using video analysis technology, make sure you and your coach or your parent know why you are doing it. Knowing your intention with video recording is the correct starting point.

There are several facets to videoing during practice that are very important. It's important to know if you are trying to evaluate technique, tactic or even the mental side of your game. Technique can involve footwork, backswing, contact point, forward swing and finish. This way, when you do things like slow it down or freeze frame a video, remember points on the screen you and your coach observe so you know what you are trying to correct. Also, once your coach sees you are starting to hit the shot correctly based on the right technique, make sure you also understand by seeing a new video what you are doing right.

As a coach make sure what you are videoing lines up with the goals of the player. We both remember learning, during our USTA High Performance programs, the importance of using video analysis to help our students with the primary foci of improvement laid out in the students' development plan.

You can also use video technology for inspirational reasons. If your coach videos parts of your match, then see if he/she can put together highlights of your best points. You could watch them for inspiration and encouragement right before you go to play your next match. We have found this to be uplifting for our players to get them focused on two things – **a positive mindset and seeing themselves hit great shots.**

When you video record, make sure you know these important factors – when, why and how? When is this player hitting the shot? This means understanding, for example, that if a player is hitting a groundstroke, the video should tell you if the player is in the back, middle or front part of the court. Why is the player hitting the shot? This means the video should make it clear what situation the player is responding to from the opponent in a match or coach in practice. So, for example, it should be apparent if the player is receiving a serve, groundstroke, volley or overhead. Finally, how is the player hitting the shot? While this might seem obvious, let's assume the video gets everything but the player's footwork. If that is the case, then the player has no idea if he/she was hitting from open, semi-open, square and closed stance. This means to position your camera so you can see the whole court. Video analysis is of no value to the player if all three items are not seen.

We have learned through our USTA High Performance training and other continuing education programs that video analysis is great for match charting. The technology will only continue to get better in this regard. We have used video match charting numerous times with our players. It is a great tool.

Finally, parents, let your kids know if you are going to video record their matches and make sure they are okay with it. In some instances, you as the parents are doing it to help the coach because the coach can't be at the match. However, we have seen too many times when parents with good intentions might want to video record their child in a lesson or match, and the child gets nervous and frustrated with the parents doing it. As we've said before, remember to be "low positive parents."

Summary

So, in conclusion, we certainly see the value of video/technology in training, but please use it wisely.

Point 4
Athlete Based Foundation

Physical On-Court Competencies

"As human beings, our greatness lies not so much in being able to remake the world, as in being able to remake ourselves."
Mahatma Gandhi

We have been fortunate through our experience as coaches to understand that all tennis player are athletes first when they compete. Their athletic skills help them become great tennis players. We want to make one thing clear from the beginning of this chapter: improving as a tennis player means doing activities without a racquet in your hand as much as with a racquet in your hand. We hope parents reading this chapter will keep an open mind when your children are developing their tennis games. We have seen too many times and made the mistake ourselves of thinking the only way players can "get better" is with a racquet in their hand. Some of the best drills a coach can do are off court drills. In this chapter, we will discuss core athletic attributes such as agility, balance, and coordination.

Without these core athletic abilities of agility, balance, and coordination tennis players will have trouble forming proper technique or tactics. These core athletic abilities help with judgment and anticipation of the ball – two key components of receiving a tennis ball. Let's relate this to ice hockey for a minute. Professional hockey players need to have two skills to be successful – ice skating and hockey stick skills. In the same way, tennis players need the two skills of footwork and correct racquet swing paths to be successful on the court. We both remember growing up as juniors doing agility, balance and coordination games that we still use today with the juniors we coach. Some of these games are ultimate tennis (ultimate Frisbee with a tennis ball), z-ball or medicine ball keep away, partner ball drops, "catch me if you can" with a Velcro tether, line tag and team "break the chain."

Let's first review what **agility, balance, and coordination** mean in general.

Agility – Agility is defined as the ability to move quickly and easily (http://www.dictionary.com/browse/agility)

Balance – Balance is the ability to stay in control of your body movements and keeping your body parts under control (https://www.topendsports.com/fitness/balance.htm). In tennis, there is static balance and dynamic balance, both of which are both important. Static balance refers to maintaining equilibrium while one is stationary. Dynamic balance means maintaining your equilibrium while you are moving on the court (https://www.topendsports.com/fitness/balance.htm).

Coordination – Coordination refers to the organization of the different elements of a complex body or activity enabling them to work together effectively in a match (https://www.merriam-webster.com/dictionary/coordination).

So, remember, these athletic competencies will not only make you a better player but help you enjoy the game more and increase your self-confidence on the court.

Before we touch on athletic competency principles for junior players of all levels, we would like to talk about our core philosophy regarding the ball progression from red to orange to green and finally yellow for 10 and under players. **We fully support it.** Our aim is not to regurgitate all the nuts and bolts that have been laid out about 10 and under development but bring up what we feel is important about the process. There is already great material available on this topic from several organizations such as USTA, USPTA and PTR and others which we recommend all coaches read to be as knowledgeable as possible.

In addition to supporting 10 and under development, we believe that playing other sports or doing other physical activities helped us when we were juniors and has helped the junior tennis players we coach. While growing up, we played soccer, baseball, basketball and other sports early on which helped develop our athletic base before we specialized in tennis. So, yes, we are saying there is a benefit to playing other sports early on and specializing later in tennis. Of course, we are biased! We hope players will choose tennis in the end as their true love. While a young player participating in tennis three times a week helps a coach with the number of lessons taught and club growth, in the short term it can be a killer for that player's long-term love of the sport and retention for playing for life. So, if any player, especially 10 and under, is going to do this, the drive to train this much must come from player first, not the coach or the parent. We only pursue this approach ourselves with a player if the player him/herself is the one who brings it up.

The athletic development of players in tennis should be thought of in the same way people achieve certain level belts in the martial arts. Each belt is a recognition that a person has achieved a certain athletic competency and mental maturity to move on to the next belt. We believe that the same mindset can be applied to moving players up to the next color tennis ball. We only move players up if they have achieved athletic competency in grips, swing paths, preparation, and footwork. We are grateful for the coaching curriculum and guidelines provided by USTA Net Generation, USTA High Performance, USPTA and PTR and other accredited organizations to help foster the fundamental and appropriate long-term development of players. We believe the actions of jumping, running, throwing and other athletic movements are vital for any junior player, especially those who are 10 and under. Our involvement in these organizations helps us continue to understand how to coach this age group better and is another reason we advocate the certification of tennis teaching professionals.

Dean Hollingworth, a world-class expert on fitness related to tennis and other sports, will in the next chapter discuss the importance of fitness in the development of a tennis player. He has over twenty-five years' experience in the health and fitness industry. He is a noted author, speaker, fitness, and performance consultant and a Master Tennis Performance Specialist in the International Tennis Performance Association. We are very grateful to have his insight in this area.

Developing Agility, Speed, Balance, and Coordination for Tennis Players

Dean Hollingworth

I have been a strength and conditioning coach for over 20 years. I've had the pleasure of working with tennis players of all levels, from juniors to the professional ranks. One of the most common conversations that I have with parents goes something like this:

> Parent: We would like you to work with our child.
> Me: Great! What are you looking for exactly?
> Parent: He/she needs better first step acceleration and needs to be more athletic on the court with his/her movement. He/she also needs better leg and core strength.
> Me: OK. I can help with that. How old is your child?
> Parent: 14 years old
> Me: Has he/she played other sports or has been doing any other type of exercise besides tennis?
> Parent: Not really, mainly on the court with a coach or friends and plays in tournaments.

What most parents or coaches don't know (or perhaps ignore) is that a child's athleticism is truly dependent upon how much exposure that child gets to the 5 S's of training: **strength, speed, suppleness, skill, and stamina**. According to the Long-Term Athletic Development (LTAD), sensitive periods occur for each one of these characteristics at early ages. Take speed for example, where these sensitive periods occur between the ages of seven and nine years for boys and even earlier for girls between the ages of six and eight years. If we take the above conversation, this first sensitive period most likely has been missed. What occurs during these sensitive periods is accelerated responsiveness of the body to training. This is not to say that an athlete cannot be made if this period is missed but think of it like this: if you had a white canvas and all the colors at your disposal, missing a sensitive period will take a few colors away. You can still paint a beautiful picture, but it may be lacking from perfection. Speed does have a second window of sensitivity between the ages of 13 and 16 for boys and between the ages of 11 and 13 for girls.

After having said all this, the answer is not to employ a performance coach for your 8-year-old athlete. Allowing your children to be introduced to many sports at a young age will enable them to explore the many different facets that make up an athlete. Sure, you want tennis to be the main component, but it can't be the only one. It is not a coincidence that the best young athletes that I have worked with, regarding movement, played soccer. Exposing your child to these sensitive periods will have a positive lasting effect.

Where do I start? What should I do? When having a child participate in fitness, it does not always have to be organized. Unless there is a coach, kids don't seem to interact on an athletic level. With younger juniors (6-9 years old), games can have an enormous impact on physical literacy, not to mention increasing social abilities. Games like tag, pitch, and catch, relay races, bulldog, ultimate Frisbee (with a Frisbee or tennis ball) are a few great examples. From my personal experience, what has also worked best with juniors is small groups (4-6 people) going through an array of activities. My primary goal when coaching juniors is not to make them better tennis players but to make them better athletes. In return, yes, you will have a well-rounded athlete who is excelling at tennis.

There is an important principle that I would like to put forth to make these "fitness" sessions for a younger junior athlete worthwhile and meaningful. It must be fun! If the kids are not having fun, it will become meaningless to them. If you keep the training dynamic and fun, you will be able to keep their full attention. This means keeping the training light with small amounts of correction, changing the drills frequently and being upbeat and passionate.

For the middle-aged junior (10-12 years old), an overall structure can now be added to this fitness component. This athlete should be made aware of proper warm-up and stretch protocols. This will not only help in setting up good future habits but will also help with physical preparation before practice and matches and will assist with recovery. An aspect that is very important to keep in mind is that a warmup must be more than just jogging around a court. A well-constructed warmup will assist in the development of the athletes on all levels (**speed, coordination, suppleness, agility, strength, and injury prevention**). Do not miss out on these 10-15 minutes. They can amount to a significant portion of physical development.

What is sometimes difficult with this age group, as can be with the others, is the difference in maturity between the young athletes. Some will be more mature and ready to take on more tasks. It is with this age group that I start directing the athletes more concerning correction of movement. When coaching athletes of any age, it is essential to use words that are rich in their descriptive nature. Words and phrases that are descriptive provide external cues that allow athletes to envision what is being asked, like "drive through the ground," "take off like a plane." Some athletes respond well to a visual demonstration. This is good if the person demonstrating is efficient at the movement being taught. Naturally, demonstrating the wrong mechanics will lead to poor performance.

Making sure the different drills and activities are constantly changing will keep them challenging and more fun resulting in a better-developed athlete. Training without meaning and purpose will result in time not well spent. Once an athlete has adapted to an exercise or drill, it is essential to move on and not stagnate. Repeating the same drill over and over becomes dull and monotonous, putting an end to physical development.

At this point in an athlete's development, learning the fundamental movements of strength training is very important. One of the primary reasons for injuries in the gym is due to lack of proper lifting technique. Now, I am not saying that a 12-year-old should load up an Olympic bar for squats. I am suggesting that perfect technique be taught for basic exercise (such as squats, lunges, push-ups, planks) so that when they do reach an age when weight training can begin, their fundamental skills are present and ready to be challenged. Lastly, rubber tubing is a great tool that can be used for other exercises and offer light resistance.

With the late juniors (13 years old and up), this is the time to start putting all the aspects of fitness together. It is time to introduce true acceleration and speed drills, plyometrics and weight training.

As is the case with any age group, a progression of the exercises is of great importance. With the likes of YouTube and other social media platforms, much information is out there on training. Unfortunately, most of it is inaccurate and can lead to injury. Take box jumps for example, where people are trying to jump as high as they can on to boxes. The boxes should not be used to show off, where the athlete's knees are practically in their ears.

Using resistance for increasing sprinting ability is a great tool when used correctly. Putting resistance on someone that has bad mechanics will lead to bad mechanics that have been reinforced. Using it to teach ground reaction force or a proper lean during acceleration is extremely beneficial. The same goes for the weight room. Young athletes sometimes get caught up with how much weight they are training with or with beach muscles. In the gym, it is imperative that proper technique be used rather than adding more weight. Also, for tennis players, the need for bigger biceps and chest is not important. The muscles in the back of our body are truly what creates a powerful tennis player.

On the next page you will find some of the top exercises and key principles for developing an athlete effectively. You will notice that most weight training exercises for the legs are performed on one leg. After perfecting the basics, I believe this is the way to go for better tennis performance. Let's be honest and realize that performing many of the skills and movement needed to be successful at tennis are performed mainly off of one leg.

Warm up
- Inchworm
- Bear crawl
- World's greatest stretch

Speed/acceleration
- Skips
- Falling starts
- Half-kneeling starts
- Resisted starts

Weight training
- Pull-ups
- One arm row
- Reverse lunges
- Bulgarian split squats
- Single leg RDL
- Glute/hamstring raises

Plyometrics
- Learning to land
- Box jumps
- Single jump forward and laterally
- Squat jumps with med ball overhead release
- Med ball throws

Agility
- High knees over hurdles, front and sideways
- Sprinting and changing direction at cones
- Shuffling and crossing over between cones
- Tennis specific movement patterns without a racquet

My **five key fitness principles**:
1) Never substitute more weight for technique.
2) Research shows that more than a 10% increase in load per week can lead to a higher rate of injury.
3) Allow ample time for recovery in between speed and agility drills. Otherwise, it becomes a conditioning drill.
4) Perform speed and power drills when the athletes are fresh, preferably before practice.
5) The warm-up and recovery portions of your program are one of the keys to injury prevention.

Summary

It is difficult to sum up a complete guide to junior athletic development in a chapter. However, the thoughts and guidelines put forth here are of extreme importance. It's just a matter of inserting the pieces to make it run. They are the building blocks for all tennis players. Without this solid foundation, your junior tennis players may not achieve the optimal level of tennis that they desire. The long-term goal is for your players to achieve their optimal level of athleticism in a progressive, efficient and safe manner.

Dean Hollingworth Bio

With over twenty-five years of experience as a strength and conditioning coach, Dean has established himself as a highly regarded author, speaker, and fitness and performance consultant. He is a Certified Strength and Conditioning Specialist, a Master Tennis Performance Specialist by the International Tennis Performance Association and part of Team PTR. He has recently published the Baselinepower video series, which addresses all aspects of fitness training for tennis players. Dean is currently the Director of fitness and sports performance at Club Sportif Cote-de-Liesse in Montréal, where he works primarily with high-performance tennis players. He has worked with all levels of tennis players including, ITF, ATP and WTA players that have included a

Grand Slam champion and Olympic gold medalist. Dean's work with world-class athletes has given him a deep understanding of the requirements and balance for high performance, helping the athletes he works with to develop all facets of athleticism. Further information on Dean can be found at www.baselinepower.com.

Good Techniques Equal Good Tactics

"I tell a student that the most important class you can take is technique. A great chef is first a great technician. If you are a jeweler, or a surgeon or a cook, you have to know the trade in your hand. You have to learn the process. You learn it through endless repetition until it belongs to you."
Jacques Pepin, French Chef

Now that we have discussed the athletic attributes that create the foundation for tennis players, we will examine how proper techniques equal good tactics. Our goal with this chapter is to lay out some principles we see that are important with technique, particularly regarding different styles of technique, related to varying tactics and situations. We are aware of the many resources out there on this subject. So, we hope you use from this chapter what helps you the most. Our thoughts on this subject come from our high-performance continuing education training, other training, and observations through years of coaching. We are grateful for our coaching mentors who have taken the time to go over this topic and help us understand it more thoroughly.

To give you an idea of our thoughts on how to relate techniques and tactics, let's take the aspects of forehands for Jack Sock, Roger Federer, and Rafael Nadal. Jack Sock's non-dominant hand sometimes falls to his side when turning for his backswing, but then does come back up with his left hand on the throat of the racquet on his unit turn. On the other hand, Nadal and Federer keep their non-dominant hand on the racquet the whole time when taking it back for a unit turn. Is either one wrong, or right? The answer is neither one is wrong or right. It's a style they use that works for them but does not affect them as world-class players. What is the common parameter for all three of these players? It's the load and the unit turn on the forehand.

Players sometimes fall into the trap of trying to adopt a **style** that a certain pro uses without knowing why. Let's look at one example with Rafael Nadal. When Rafael first came on the scene, some coaches including us at first were teaching the Rafa buggy whip forehand finish as a main part of the swing instead of a stylistic or situational choice. This type of forehand swing helps with defense shots and adds RPMs (Revolutions per minute) to his shots.

Let's look at the same principle with the serve regarding grips. Stefan Edberg and Boris Becker had very different grips on their serves, but both had world class serves that helped them win multiple Wimbledon championships. Edberg's grip was more toward eastern backhand, and Becker's grip was eastern forehand. So, if you're trying to copy a world class player, which grip should you use? The key is to use the one that works best for you!

The critical concept here is that even though these players' forehands and serves are very different, they are still able to execute the right tactics for successful shots under pressure. Two questions you should ask about techniques are these: does the technique help you **(1) hit the shot you want to hit and (2) not cause long-term injury.** The main point we are making here is that proper techniques do need to fall into acceptable parameters but don't need to be the same to correlate to good tactics.

As we elaborate on how good techniques equal good tactics, it's important to remember as you are learning the main strokes in tennis that they should generally correlate with good athletic technique. Below is a chart explaining the main strokes and what athletic technique correlates with each one. Please keep in mind, of course, your coach's advice as you work on these techniques. This chart below is just a basis for starting.

Shot	Athletic Technique
Serve	Hail Mary Passing Motion
Overhead	Volleyball Spiking Motion
Groundstroke	Swinging (tossing a medicine ball)

| Volley | Catching/Absorbing Motion |

Before explaining each of these shots in more detail, we will first touch on the most common issues we see with grips, footwork stances, and swing paths, and how those relate to tactics or strokes being used.

Grips

Some players use semi-western, some use western, and some use eastern. None of these grips is wrong! In this book, we do not prescribe a particular grip. However, we admit that there are grip parameters that make sense depending on which stroke you're hitting. For example, continental or close to continental works best for volleys, serves, overheads and backhand slices. For forehand groundstrokes, we would say eastern to semi or full western is the best. From our continuing education and years of teaching, we believe these are the proper parameters for grips that players should use. Besides the tactics and strokes being used, players and coaches should use grips that work best for their players based on their players' playing style also.

Footwork

Here we will look at the most common footwork patterns for serves, returns of serve, volleys, overheads and baseline play and how they all relate to tactics. Our goal in this section is to point out some common things we see regarding footwork. First, know which footwork stance you are working on – **receiving, sending or recovery.** Before we go any further, let's define the main footwork stances (for the sending stage of the shot).

Open Stance – The feet and hips are aligned parallel to the net.

Semi-Open Stance – This stance ends up being between open and square stance where the feet are diagonal at a 45-degree angle relative to the net.

Square Stance – Here the two legs are lined up and are perpendicular to the net.

Closed Stance – The opposite leg has crossed over in front of the near side leg. This means that on the forehand the left leg has crossed over the right leg. Below is a visual of the four different stances for a right-handed player (tt.tenniswarehouse.com).

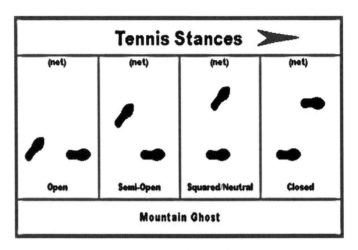

Now, we will look at the receiving and recovery footwork principles. For this part of footwork make sure you base your footwork on the athletic situation at hand: whether you need to go long distance, medium distance or short distance on the court. In general, the receiving and recovering footwork is based on the distance you need to go. For example, as coaches, we have learned you can use these rules of thumb for receiving and recovery footwork – the shorter the distance (two or three steps) you should shuffle or take adjustment steps, and the farther distance use crossover steps then run. Whatever footwork you use, make sure it matches the situation and tactic at the time.

Serve – The serve has two main footwork moves – *pinpoint* and *platform*. *Pinpoint* means the back foot comes up to front foot just before you hit the ball whereas *platform* means both feet stay back as the player hits the ball. Both are okay. Roger Federer and Pete Sampras use/used platform and Serena Williams and Stefan Edberg uses/used pinpoint. The main point is that all the players use/used one or the other stance well with winning results depending on their tactics. For example, for Edberg, the pinpoint technique was helpful in propelling him into the court so he could get to the net quickly and effectively when serving and volleying. Also, remember the serve and overhead motions are not the same as throwing a baseball but more like Hail Mary passes for the serve and Volleyball spikes for overheads.

Return of Serve –Some players like Andy Murray use a step forward and split step before receiving the serve while other players like Novak Djokovic get low and hop before receiving the serve. Both are right. They represent different styles but both players still split-step before hitting the return allowing them to be aggressive on second serves. We have seen that open stance or semi-open stance is more useful on fast-paced serves. Closed or square stance is better on a slower second serve and can be more effective for hitting offensive shots.

Volleys – You have probably heard coaches say, "volley with your feet." We certainly believe this to be the case and have said this phrase ourselves many times because we usually look at the footwork first if players have issues with their volleys. However, we want to be more specific than just "volley with your feet." With volleys, we want to touch on three main points that relate to footwork. While we certainly understand that factors affecting volley footwork can be broken down, even more, we believe these factors make the biggest difference with footwork: **the speed of the incoming ball, the height of the incoming ball, and your court positioning.**

Let's go over footwork techniques that are frequently used. One is called *flowing footwork*. This means you keep your feet moving through the shot even after contacting the ball to keep your center of gravity balanced. The other one that is also common is *v-footwork*, which is what most juniors are taught. This is when for example on the forehand volley (with a right-handed player) the left footsteps in front of the right as the player hits the ball.

If an incoming ball is slow, you should generally use the *flowing footwork*. Another footwork technique for a slow and deep ball, especially if it is shoulder height, can be a load step where you step with the outside foot first to help move through the shot.

If the ball is coming fast and you are inside the service line, then we suggest using the *v-footwork*.

The basic principle is to use the footwork technique that continues to keep **your center of gravity balanced**. Once you have the footwork part down, then the racquet work for the volley will be easier and allow you to hit the volley where you want tactically. These techniques will help you hit low volleys deep in the court and high volleys angled off the court.

Overhead – We have seen so many players miss overheads, and the first thing they look at is their racquet. While that is part of the reason players miss, the real reason probably starts with their feet and includes these footwork options (for right-handed players):
- a drop step with the right foot, then shuffle steps
- a drop step with right foot, then crossover steps
- a jab step with left foot, crossover and then run back

The farther back it is hit, the more crossover or running should be done. These techniques help players hit their overheads where they want to especially deep to the corners of the court.

Baseline Play- For baseline play, we find the following helpful for footwork and swing paths in relation to tactics and different match situations. Baseline play can be broken down into the three tactics and situations – **offense, defense, and neutral.** We understand coaches use the same or different names for these situations, but the principles still apply. For our purposes, we will use these terms.

Offense means you are in control and tactically you can take away time from your opponent, needing less time yourself to recover for the next shot. **Defense** means the opponent is in control and tactically you need more time to recover for the next shot. **Neutral** means neither player has the advantage. We are aware these are not earth-shattering or new terms for many players, but we want to be clear on what we are referencing. It is vital for players to be aware of which situation they are in to apply tactics effectively. From our experiences, the situations that can be confusing are **defense and neutral**.

Stances for Baseline Play - Different stances generally make the most sense depending on one's tactic. We will discuss this next.

Open Stance – Open stance is applied more often in **defensive** situations, especially with the forehand when hitting the ball crosscourt and needing time to recover for the next shot.

Semi-Open Stance – We find semi-open is the best stance for **neutral** or **defensive** situations when looking to push your opponent back or off the court. This is truer with the forehand than with the backhand. However, you will see high level players using this for offensive shots also.

Square Stance or Closed Stance – These stances are used with the backhand in most situations and with the forehand when looking to hit a more offensive shot when you are on balance.

Swing Path for Baseline Play – We will now discuss some common swing paths and how they correlate to tactics.

Buggy Whip Swing Path – This swing is from low to finishing high above the head on the same side of the body on which it started. This should be used more often as a tactic in defensive situations.

Bless You Swing Path – This swing starts low and finishes with the racquet over the opposite shoulder from where it started. We call it *"bless you"* swing path because your arm will generally finish in front of you like you covered your mouth to sneeze. We realize other coaches may use this term for this swing. It can be used for several situations, but more when wanting to hit a neutral shot back to your opponent. This can be the most common swing path taught by coaches and pros.

Tabletop Swing Path – This is when the ball, especially on the forehand, is high above the net and slow and the player can swing as if swinging across a tabletop finishing on the outside of the opposite shoulder, and is used more often when looking to hit an offensive shot.

Summary

Our goal in this chapter is not to say one idea is wrong or better than the other. However, it's important to understand that good technique will correlate to delivering good tactics--the ones players want to perform in a match. We hope this information provides you with simple and effective ways to tie good techniques to your tactics on the court.

Move Smarter, Not Harder

"Direction is so much more important than speed.
Many are going nowhere fast."
Anonymous

"In the midst of movement and chaos,
keep stillness inside of you."
Deepak Chopra

Many people are mesmerized by Roger Federer's beautiful swings, but the attribute that we recognize most with Federer is his movement, and we can sum it up in one phrase - "Move Smarter, not Harder." In this chapter, we want to analyze the fundamentals we see that allow him to move the way he does around the court so effortlessly. While it is true that most touring pros, in general, do the things that we will discuss, Roger does them better. You might say he looks like *poetry in motion*.

Jim Courier, former No.1, has said of Federer, "When Roger is in full flight, he looks like he is gliding. Almost like he is floating above the court." (*Federer Exerts His Power from the Ground Up*, **New York Times**, Tennis, Greg Bishop, August 30, 2009, https://www.nytimes.com/2009/08/31/sports/tennis/31feder er.html).

Furthermore, in the same article Courier mentions David Bailey, an Australian coach and footwork specialist who describes Federer's footwork this way: "Bailey contends footwork is an underdeveloped part of tennis, and in inventing *the Bailey Method*, he studied more than 30,000 clips of tennis movement. Borrowing from the instructional style of Bruce Lee, Bailey broke tennis footwork into what he called 15 contact moves—basically, athletic movement when striking the ball—and he provides a corresponding clip for each in his instructional videos. According to his research, a seasoned pro performs seven contact moves at a high level. Three are offensive moves, two defensive and two rallies. These moves define a player's style, whether as a baseliner, for example, or a clay-court specialist. Federer is the only pro Bailey studied who performs all 15 moves at a high level. If Bailey wanted, he could use Federer for each video clip."

Before we get into some of the specifics, we want to establish what we mean by "Move Smarter, Not Harder." As coaches and teaching pros, we both have been guilty of using the phrase "Move Your Feet!" with students. While a player may be needed to move with more intensity, the reality is this may not be the real problem. Self-reflecting on these times in our coaching, our player was probably not moving well enough or with enough intention because of lack of good communication by us about what we expected the player to do. Our frustration with the player at a time like this is most likely equal to the player's frustration by not understanding a general phrase like "Move Your Feet!"

So, what do we mean when we say, "Move Smarter, Not Harder"? Moving smarter means maximizing a player's athletic movements to ensure he/she is in the best-balanced position to hit the shot that will give the player the best chance to win the point based on the situation. Another way to think about this is a player who does this looks like he/she is always in the flow of the point. For example, it means not running to hit the ball when you only needed to shuffle a little to make the shot. We certainly are not implying that Roger does not "work hard." He is one of the hardest if not the hardest workers on the tour. He has just trained in a way that has made him one of the smarter movers if not the smartest mover on the tour. In this chapter, we explore moving in various situations revolving around baseline play, frontcourt (net play), serve and return of serve. This is a specific area of coaching we continue learning ourselves for the benefit of our students' enjoyment and future success. We believe continuing education in this area for coaches is essential.

Baseline Play– Federer's baseline footwork movements have a purpose and are rarely wasted. His ability to move laterally, backward, and forwards, is equally skillful and proficient.

Federer is particularly efficient with his receiving and recovery movement by shuffling, crossing over or running when needed, based on the situation. For example, utilizing shuffle steps when necessary allows him to keep his shoulders square to the net so he can change direction easier. When training your footwork, make sure you place as much importance on the movement to the ball and after the ball is hit compared to your footwork stances when striking the ball. We feel that one of the biggest mistakes players can make is overtraining the footwork stances associated with sending the ball back compared to the movement before and after striking the ball. This concept is just as important in other sports. A baseball player needs to know how to move to catch a ball, and a football player needs to move well to make an interception.

Federer's timing and the location of his split-steps are usually flawless. He split-steps shortly before his opponent strikes the ball allowing him to push off the inside leg then landing in the direction of the incoming ball. This allows him to be very pro-active in getting to the ball, so he can go for the next shot.

Federer is also a master at off-center recovery with his split-step. When he hits the ball crosscourt, he recovers off-center and split-steps to the same side on which he had been where he just hit the ball. He only recovers past the center mark and split-steps when he hits a crosscourt baseline shot from his opponent back down the line. He is doing this to ensure that he recovers to the **optimal recovery spot**—which bisects the possible angles that can come back from his opponent's next shot. These two footwork fundamentals— timing and location—are crucial to being in the prime position to anticipate the next shot. Federer is also one of the best at utilizing the drop-step movement for his forehand. The drop step move involves turning the hips and dropping the outside leg behind the body. His ability to use his large muscle groups such as his hips, core muscles, shoulders, and legs to get behind the ball allows him to hit equally well an inside-out or inside-in forehand.

He also does a great job of using his outside leg for recovering on wide defensive balls. When pushed out wide on the baseline and needing to recover from a defensive position, he does incredibly well at pushing off his outside leg to get back for the next shot. Novak Djokovic and other players also do this well.

Front Court (Net Play) – Especially as he approaches the net, Federer's timing of his split-step is very effective. Again, it usually happens when his opponent is about to hit the ball. This is important because it allows Federer to move with purpose and direction toward an incoming volley or overhead. Other great volleyers such as Patrick Rafter and Stefan Edberg also had this skill. When coaches use the phrase "great players volley with their feet" this is what they mean. The concept of "gliding" is something Federer does very well in the frontcourt.

Serve and Return of Serve – Great champions in tennis not only move their feet after the serve but do it in a way that helps them hit their favorite shot first. Roger is a master of this footwork approach in serving. It's one of the reasons he is world class at the "serve + 1 play." Landing on his right foot after completing the whole service motion, he immediately recognizes the shot coming back and knows to attack, hold or absorb it. If he realizes his opponent has hit an offensive shot straight back at him, he will take a drop step back with his right foot to create space to absorb and swing at the ball. If his opponent hits a weak return, Roger recognizes it and punishes it with a forehand winner. Rafael Nadal is very good at ball recognition after the serve also.

On the return of serve, Federer lands his split-step on the balls of his feet with a footwork base around shoulder width apart. Like Jimmy Connors and Andre Agassi, he is off the ground with his split step by the time the ball crosses the net, and he usually finishes it before the ball bounces. The excellent timing of the split-step allows these players to achieve a good start on their unit turn for forehand or backhand, allowing them to hit a more effective return.

Summary

So, if you want to play like Roger Federer and other great players start with your feet, not your racquet and "move smarter, not harder!"

Point 5
Match Day

Awareness Attributes of Champions – Singles and Doubles

"The first step toward change is awareness.
The second step is acceptance."
Nathaniel Branden

"I don't focus on what I'm up against.
I focus on my goals and I try to ignore the rest."
Venus Williams

We believe all players need to have certain awareness attributes on the court, attributes that all great champions display and are exceptionally good at. In tennis, we are talking about the awareness traits that allow players to stay focused on match day on the key elements that allow them to be successful.

Before we demonstrate awareness attributes in tennis, we'd like to start with some analogies from other areas of life. Let's take driving for example. When you are driving, you need to focus on three or four things to get you from point A to point B, which include an *awareness of your actions, other cars, the road and traffic lights*. Items like the air conditioning or the radio are just background noise that doesn't serve any purpose except for adding to the experience of driving. In short, to get from point A to point B without an accident you focus on core issues and disregard the more peripheral or tangential ones.

Think for a moment about public speaking. We have both learned from doing presentations that you need to be aware of your actions and the responses of the people you are addressing in the room or on the court. Anyone in the listening audience who might be talking or texting on a cell phone, writing down notes from your talk or nodding off (hopefully not!), although distractions to be sure cannot cause you to lose your place in your speech if you are a pro at public speaking. Interestingly, in every area of life, proper preparation makes all the difference when you are speaking, performing or playing a sport. The real champions are always prepared for whatever comes, which makes it easier and easier to focus on each shot and adjust as necessary.

Now let's go back to tennis. We believe there are two important awareness attributes for tennis players – **self-awareness and situational awareness.** In this chapter, we touch on both. Self-awareness will apply to singles and doubles. For situational awareness, we will first talk about singles and then doubles.

Self-Awareness

We begin our examination of self-awareness by looking at a couple of definitions that apply to both singles and doubles. Self-awareness is having a clear perception of your personality, including strengths, weaknesses, thoughts, emotions, motivations, anxieties and beliefs (https://www.pathwaytohappiness.com/self-awareness.htm). Self-awareness is the ability to recognize oneself as an individual separate from the environment and other individuals (https://en.wikipedia.org/wiki/Self-awareness). How do these relate to tennis? In tennis, the drive to compete must come from within the player and not anyone else. If the drive to compete comes from within, then you will know your own **strengths, weaknesses, and motivations on the court**. You could call these three qualities *the ABCs of self-awareness* on the tennis court. In all great champions like Roger Federer, Rafael Nadal, Andre Agassi, Rod Laver, the Williams Sisters, Chris Evert, Steffi Graf, and others self-awareness in strengths, weaknesses, and motivations on the court is very high. They know why they are there and what they want to do in every match based on their strengths, weaknesses, and motivations as players. In other words, they are "internally focused."

Next, we will look at **situational awareness** regarding different **phases of play**. Singles first. These ideas come from our coaching experiences and continuing education as we incorporate the terms we have mentioned in previous chapters.

Playing Phase Awareness - Singles

Serving – We associate five phases with serving in the context of "serve plus one" (responding to the return of the opponent). They include **serve and defend, serve and hold, serve and attack, serve and sneak attack, and serve and volley.** There are others that you and your coach might work on, but we think these are the main five. First, let's define each situation.

Serve and defend means the opponent has taken control of the point with his/her return and put the server on defense.

Serve and hold means that after the return both players are in neutral.

Serve and sneak attack means the server was not intending to serve and volley but has seen the opportunity to take a weak return from the opponent out of the air to gain an advantage.

Serve and attack means the server comes in to hit a groundstroke approach shot after he/she serves.

Serve and volley means player serves and volleys with the intention of doing that regardless of the return.

It's important for players to understand these "serving plus one" and other phases so that they can apply corresponding footwork stances, shot selection and other actions based on the situation. Some of the items mentioned in this chapter, we discussed in the good techniques equal good tactics chapter. For example, if a player is in the *serve and defend* situation after his/her serve with the ball going deep to the forehand, then the player might want to crossover and run back to the ball to load better on the outside leg and hit it with a semi-open stance or open stance for better recovery for next shot.

Return of Serve – Here we talk about three main phases – **survive, neutralize, and gain advantage.** *Survive* means the opponent has you totally off balance because of his/her serve and therefore is in control of the point. *Neutralize* means the serve has moved you along the baseline and you're trying to keep the other player in neutral. *Gain advantage* means you are going to be able to get your way with a shot that is in your optimum strike zone where you can now take control of the point with your return.

Baseline – In general, we have learned that players can divide the baseline play up into three phases - **attack, hold, or absorb (or defend).** We have learned about these through USPTA, PTR and USTA High Performance continuing education.

These three phases rely on the three main items – *balance when striking the ball, court position* (which zone of the court when striking the ball, which we will discuss shortly) and *optimal strike zone when hitting the ball* (between waist and shoulder), in other words, one's wheelhouse. **Attack** means all three are in your favor. **Hold** means two are in your favor. **Absorb** means none is in your favor.

Court positioning and taking away time from your opponent are also important aspects of each of these phases. As a player, it can be as simple as knowing if these aspects are in your favor or not. Below is a chart explaining this from your perspective in contrast to your opponent.

	Court Position (in your favor?)	Taking Away Time (in your favor?)
Attack	Yes	Yes
Hold	Even	Even
Defend	No	No

The awareness of the baseline playing phase affects four main ball control components – **ball speed, ball height, ball depth, and ball directions.** We will explain each one. Finally, players can apply these factors to the return of serve also with **survive** equaling **absorb**, **hold** equaling neutralize and **attack** equaling **gain advantage**.

Ball speed – Ball speed means the responding pace off your racquet back to your opponent in contrast to the speed of the ball your opponent hit to you.

Ball Height – Ball Height means the height over the net at which you hit the ball back to your opponent. In coaching, we use three heights. Each represents a certain amount of racquet lengths from the butt cap to the head of the racquet. The higher the number, the more racquets. So, height 3 equals three racquets, height 2 equals two racquets, and height 1 equals one racket. So, to determine the ball height, use your racquet and figure the formula from there.

Ball Depth – Ball depth refers to where the first bounce of the ball lands when sent to the other side. In our coaching, we use the different zones of the court. From our continuing education, we have learned to use 6 zones – which are divided up into six equal parts from the net to the back curtain with one being closest to the net and six being farthest from the net.

Ball Direction – Ball direction means whether you are hitting crosscourt or down the line. There are other ball direction patterns, but we will stick these for now.

Below is a simple **baseline decision-making chart** we like to use for this. This chart needs to be used in the context of two players in a baseline crosscourt rally. As players get more advanced, they can start to do more advanced patterns such as inside-out forehand and then inside-in forehand.

Baseline Decision-Making Chart

Phase of Play	Ball Speed	Ball Height	Ball Depth	Ball Direction
Attack	Increase	Height 1	Zone 4	Down the line
Hold	Same	Height 2 or 3	Zone 3 or 4	Crosscourt pushing person back or off the court
Absorb	Slower	Height 3	Zone 4	Crosscourt

Net play – With net play we will discuss two main phases concerning singles– **you are coming into the net, or your opponent is coming into the net.**

Each phase of net play can be broken down into two roles – **the attacker or the reactor.**

You are coming into the net - If you are the **attacker**, it means you are choosing to come in and hitting your shot on balance. If you are the **reactor**, then you are coming in only because your opponent has forced you in and you are more than likely off balance when hitting the shot. As the attacker you are positioned to take control of the point, so hit into the open court with a groundstroke, overhead or volley or hit a drop shot. If you are the reactor, then you might need to hit your first volley or overhead after your groundstroke approach shot deep in the court and keep it in front of you to get set up to hit an offensive shot on next ball.

Opponent coming to the net - However, what about your opponent coming to the net? The opponent is now either the attacker or the reactor. If the opponent is the **attacker**, and you are the **reactor**, then you have these main options – hit a groundstroke high (lob) or hit low to set up a passing shot. If you are the reactor, then you need time to prepare for the next shot. If your opponent is a reactor, and you are the attacker, then you can try hitting a passing shot or an offensive lob.

Doubles – Playing Phase Awareness

We will now look at doubles. While several principles can be applied to doubles the same way, they are applied to singles there are some differences which we will cover now.

Let's first look at the playing phases regarding *offense, defense, and neutral*. The concept is similar, but the main difference has to do with how you as a team are you situated on the court in contrast to the opposing team. For example, if both teams are *one up and one back* then both teams are in neutral. It is not until you (as teammates) are *both up or both back* that you are in offense or defense. The best position to be in statistically speaking is *both up and in balance* to hit volleys or overheads. This formation puts your team in an offensive position to take charge and win the point. You can be *on offense* when you are both back, but it's much harder to win the point in this formation.

Doubles – Role Awareness

Let's now look at each role in doubles - **server, server's partner, returner and returner's partner.**

It is imperative that the four roles of doubles be understood because unlike team sports such as soccer, baseball, football, hockey, or basketball, you are not possibly training or specializing in one position for match day. In tennis, you want to understand and be good at all four. Yes, every player has a strength and might be better at serving than returning or vice versa but the Bryan Brothers (the most successful doubles team in history) have taken the approach of loving each role and being good at each one. Seems to pay off for them! Even when Rafael Nadal and Roger Federer play doubles, they understand this principle about the four roles. The reality is in doubles you will have to play all four positions, like it or not!

Roles in Serving Phase – We touched on this some in a previous chapter highlighting the importance of having a high percentage on the first serve. So, for the server in this phase, you could think of this person as having to be the *steady initiator* for starting the point. The server's first focus should be to get as many first serves in as possible to the opponent's weaker returning side.

The server's partner is like a *goaltender, disrupter, or the poacher* (which we will discuss further in another chapter). The server's partner is a *goaltender* because a ball that is hit one or two steps from server's partner is one you can volley back, hopefully into the open court. The server's partner is a *disrupter* because if that player can disrupt the returner's return by faking a poach with one step to the middle and then back quickly. Finally, the server's partner is a *poacher*, which means that the player recognizes a weak shot hit by the returner allowing him/her to move over and intercept what would typically be the server's shot.

Roles in the Receiving Phase - The receiver is the *reactor* or the *attacker*. While we realize this can be broken down more specifically, we think this is a good basis to start. The returner serves as a *reactor* because when a good serve has been hit the returner's job is to get the ball back to give your team a chance.

The goal is to hit this ball crosscourt away from the net player unless the returner is pulled way wide and has an easy topspin shot down the line in the alley. The returner is an *attacker* because the return can be hit aggressively, leading to more options—an aggressive crosscourt return, a lob over the net person, or a short angle drop shot.

The receiver's partner (the hardest position) is an *enforcer*, *absorber* or *last resort*. He/she is an *enforcer* because his/her partner has hit a shot that creates an opportunity for him/her to move from the service line to hit the ball into an open court for a winner or crippling shot. He/she is an *absorber* because his/her partner has hit a shot that the server's partner can volley aggressively which he/she has to absorb thus holding his/her ground. He/she is the *last resort* if the receiver is pulled way off the court causing the returner's partner to cover the middle of the court as a last resort for that team staying in the point.

Summary

Our goal with this chapter was not to attempt to explain every in and out of this topic but to make you aware of the important awareness attributes that will help you be successful in both singles and doubles matches.

Being a Problem Solver on the Court

"A problem is a chance for you to do your best."
Duke Ellington

Any tennis champion has the quality of being a problem solver on the court. The reality is that problem solving should be part of what all coaches teach you whether you are a club level player, college player, or pro. Through our tennis journeys, this is the aspect and challenge we have enjoyed most about tennis. In this chapter, we will discuss a system for problem-solving during the match from the second you walk on the court with your opponent to when you shake hands at the end of the match.

It starts with understanding that your role as a player, to give yourself the best chance to win, is like being a detective solving a case. A system or process helps create clarity on how a player should move through the potential whirlwind mindset of a match. It can be broken down into these specific phases – **gathering data, sampling and analyzing the data** and **closing the case.**

Before we discuss these three areas, we want to point out that players need three foci when they step on the court for a match to be effective problem solvers. They include **footwork focus, mental focus, and competitive focus.** *Footwork focus* means they are treating every ball like a "match ball" not a warmup ball. They view getting to the ball balanced and with the right contact as just as important in warmup as in the match. Jeremy's dad always used to tell him to "win the warmup **with your feet.**" *Mental focus* means focusing on only three things - you, your opponent and the ball. *Competitive focus* means the player understands that the competition starts as soon as his/her feet step on the court.

Gathering Data – One of the best ways to problem solve is to be as proactive as possible. Why is this important? It's simple! Think about it. If you start losing points, instead of feeling helpless, you have a way based on simple data to get you back in the match. Too often we see junior players let problems come to them when, if they had taken some proactive steps, then the problem might never have surfaced.

This starts with gathering data shortly before the first ball is struck and during the warm-up. Before you hit the first ball see if your opponent is a right-hander or a southpaw. We always find it interesting when a junior comes off the court with no idea whether he/she was playing a lefty or a righty. During the warm-up, make sure you are paying attention to what shot your opponent likes to hit when the ball goes down the middle, what type of movement your opponent is good at, which volley the opponent hits better at the net, or what kind of serves your opponent hits during the warmup—flat or spin.

Sampling and Analyzing the Data – Once you have gathered the data then decide on a plan to sample the data. When using this approach make sure it revolves around a serve, return of serve, baseline or net play strategy. For example, let's say you have warmed up and noticed that your opponent has a weak backhand. His/her home base is moving along the baseline, and he/she barely hits shots at the net during the warmup. How do you use the data you've gathered to sample it? Based on this information, we would suggest hitting some balls deep to your opponent's backhand but then, after couple of shots, hit a mid-court shot initially short to pull the opponent up to what may be an uncomfortable position causing an error or opening the court up for you to hit an offensive shot, either crosscourt or down the line.

Now let's analyze the data. It can be done straightforwardly. As you implement the strategy, take note if you are winning points or games from using the strategy. If it is working, then you have a successful strategy! If not, you may need to reevaluate and recalibrate.

During this stage of problem-solving, it is vital to distinguish between "pivot" moments and "outlier" moments. "Pivot moments" mean your opponent has won enough points that warrant you to reassess your strategy. "Outlier moments" mean your opponent has won a couple of points but has not shown it to be a sustainable strategy for coming back. Great champions always correctly recognize these moments during a match. If it is an "outlier" moment, then continue with your strategy. If it is a "pivot" moment, you will need to reboot and move on to another strategy.

Closing the Case – Now that you have gathered the data and correctly sampled and analyzed the data it is time to close the case. This means continue your strategy and focus as if they were the only three things in the world right now - *you, the opponent and the ball*.

Summary

Problem-solving is a vital skill on match day. We hope this process is helpful to you. Why not try it in your next match?

Mastering the Tiebreak

"I should have closed the first set in the tiebreak earlier than I did, but I tried to stay positive all the way through, and I think that was the difference between us today."
Radek Stepanek

"I think that's why I play tennis, because of the challenge, because of the competition...That's why we love to play the tiebreak in the third set."
Maria Sharapova

"In the tiebreak, I decided not to come off the court saying *I could have gone for a bit more* and with regrets, so in a few points, I went for some big shots, and it paid off."
Andy Murray

Why a whole chapter on the tiebreak? There are two main reasons: (a) it is not practiced enough, and (b) it can be the most stressful part of the match because it can be a closeout moment for one player and a momentum shifter for the other one. These factors apply to singles and doubles play. Our goal in this chapter is not to cover the way to play a tie-break, but the things you need to consider to be successful in one.

We start with the fact that tiebreaks may be the part of tennis that is practiced the least when it highlights some key characteristics that every great champion needs to have to win—resiliency and focus. Because of that, we have seen the value of practicing tiebreaks in clinics, especially before a tournament by doing round-robin tiebreak shoot-outs where the person with the most points at the end wins. Also, as a player, remember to practice tiebreaks so when you're in a match you are not trying to figure who serves first, where to serve, how many serves you have, when to switch ends, and so on. All those questions should be answered in practice so that playing a tiebreak becomes almost second nature to you.

So, what do we view as the most important way to be successful in a tiebreak? There are three main components –**using geometric strategies, being positive, and using your strengths**. You could consider this the **GPS strategy** of tiebreaks. To put this in the right perspective, this philosophy is particularly important when you as the player are trying to shift the momentum back in your favor, but these are also important when as a player you are in *closeout mode* finishing a set or the match.

Using geometric strategies - The first component of being successful in tiebreaks is using geometric strategies. This means basing your shot selection on the geometry of the court. For example, if you are on defense hitting the ball from behind the baseline, send your next shot the longest direction on the court which based on geometry would be crosscourt. If you have climbed your way back in the set by using the geometry of the court more effectively then **keep doing it!** The different playing styles of your opponents, the wind, sun and other items, may vary, but the dimensions of a tennis court will always be the same.

Being positive –A positive mindset is necessary because there's no room in a tiebreak for negative thoughts that distract you from moving your feet and hitting the shots that need to be executed. Any time we as coaches can help a player in a tiebreak, we always start with the player's mental state first. Remember you can still win even if you're down 6-3 or 6-2, so **never give up!**

Using your strengths – We both had times in our junior playing days when we turned around a match in a tiebreak by staying positive and going to back to using our strengths to attack the other player's weaknesses. Even if we lost, we left the court knowing we did all we could to turn it around.

Summary

Make sure you remember to employ principles for success—mentally and tactically—every time you play a tiebreak.

Being Smarter Than the Cheater

"Cheaters never win, and winners never cheat."
Andrew Keane

We wish we could say this chapter is unnecessary and that all tennis players are so ethical that they never cheat. However, the reality is this not the case. Unfortunately, in all areas of life, cheating exists. Especially at a young age, players need to know a system and a process for how to deal with cheating. This is what we will discuss in this chapter.

Let's start first with the idea that we never cheat. Really? We both know there have been times we have cheated on an opponent with a line call without even realizing it. So, let's be honest and recognize that your opponent might view you as a cheater as much as you think your opponent is.

Second, if someone does cheat on you whether it be with a line call or the score then what is the point of getting mad? You might say, "Well certain players have gotten mad like John McEnroe or Jimmy Connors." But we think for those players it was a form of release from their thinking about the bad line call. We would argue, however, that for most players getting mad makes things worse. The bigger problem with getting mad is the reality you can't change the call by getting angry about it. The only way the call can be reversed is if an official happened to be standing on the court when the bad line call was made. Then it can be corrected.

Third, as a player, you need to know why the other player might be doing this? Here is the good news. It usually is because that player is trying to hide a weakness that you have exploited. Either way, this a good situation to be in.

Fourth, realize that players who make it a habit of cheating will not succeed in the long term in tennis. As they improve their games and possibly move up to higher levels in tournament play, eventually there will be officials making the calls and or better players will figure out strategies to take away the cheating as an advantage. So, what does all this mean? It means that in the first instance of cheating that you experience as a player you have a choice. You can either hold onto the frustration or let it go and figure out a solution.

So, what are some solutions to dealing with cheaters? First, kindly ask your opponent if he/she is sure your shot was out. If the answer is yes, ask them no further questions. Go back and get ready to serve, return or switch sides and forget about it.

Second, if you're playing a point and it happens again, ask him/her one more time to see if he/she responds the same way. If the response is the same, respectfully say that you are going to request an official if one is close by. If an official is around, then you are part of the way there. While getting the official is a good step you still need to take your mind off the bad line call. Once the official is there, forget about it and play the match. If another questionable line call occurs, the official is there to overrule it. If you are winning, then keep following your strategy; but if you're losing, move your frustration to focus on a new strategy. One approach might be to take your opponent out of his/her comfort zone. So, for example, if your opponent likes to move along the baseline, hit some balls well within the court and just past service line. We like to call these "teaser shots." Now by doing this, your mind is not on the cheating. If no official is around, then take the same positive approach with no official present. Often, we have seen juniors, and experienced players have their minds clouded by cheaters when they should focus on what matters in a match.

Summary

Sadly, you will experience cheaters somewhere along the line in your playing journey. So, the best thing you can do is not to get mad but have a process for handling it. Remember, one of the primary life skills tennis teaches is handling conflict logically and peacefully. For further reference, here's an excellent online article on this subject: http://www.expert-tennis-tips.com/cheating-in-tennis.html

Using Strategic Patterns for Doubles Success

"What I found over the years is the most important thing is for a team to come together over a compelling vision, a comprehensive strategy for achieving that vision, and then a relentless implementation plan."
Alan Mulally
Former CEO of Ford Motor Company

In the next couple of chapters, we will discuss doubles themes and principles that we feel are very important to that part of a tennis player's journey. We will start with a story from USTA High Performance continuing education training.

Picture it now. It was early afternoon on July 16, 2016, in Portland, OR at the Tualatin Hills Tennis Center. The United States Davis Cup team was feeling good after winning both their first two singles matches the day before in dramatic fashion against the Croatian Davis Cup team. The USA and Croatia were playing each other in the Davis Cup World Group Quarter Final. The winner would be playing the winner of Argentina vs. Great Britain.

In the first rubber, American Jack Sock was playing a top ten player in the world, the number one Croatian player and the 2014 US Open Champion Marin Cilic. Sock, after falling behind two sets to Cilic, roared back to win the next three sets in a row in a thrilling five-set victory for the hometown crowd. It was a particularly tough loss for Cilic after just a couple of weeks earlier being ahead of Roger Federer in the Wimbledon quarterfinal by two sets and losing in five sets. In the second rubber American John Isner, feeling the momentum from the Sock win and the energy of the hometown crowd, beat Croatian Borna Coric in three sets utilizing his big serve to his advantage.

At the time, we were involved in a continuing education USTA High Performance Workshop on professional patterns of play held in conjunction with the Davis Cup match. We were with 20 other coaches selected from the across the county. This workshop, which was an incredible experience, included being able to see the Davis Cup teams practice and being involved in discussions with Jay Berger, one of the US Davis Cup coaches and former top ten ATP player. We remember leaving the Hotel Vintage Portland in downtown Portland where our morning discussions were being held to head to the Tualatin Hills Tennis Center about 20 minutes' drive from the Hotel and being very confident about the prospects of the US wrapping up the tie that day with the Bryan Brothers playing that afternoon.

The Bryan Brothers were up against Marin Cilic and Ivan Dodig. Marian Cilic is a former grand slam champion, and Ivan Dodig is a one of the world's best doubles players. The stadium was brimming with excitement with everyone thinking, "How could the Bryan Brothers lose in this situation? They are at home; the momentum is with them, and they are the Bryan Brothers!"

While the Bryan Brothers had definite advantages going into the match, two factors ended up playing a big role in the outcome. One was the history of Dodig against the Bryan Brothers. Dodig with Marcelo Melo won his first grand slam doubles title against the Bryan Brothers at the 2015 French Open. Tim, other coaches and I knew he understood how to win against the Bryan Brothers. With the excitement of the moment, it was easy to overlook that fact at the time.

Second, Marin Cilic was Dodig's partner even though he was not supposed to play. Marin Draganja was originally in the line-up. However, after the Croatians got down 0-2 following the first two rubbers, the Croatian coaching staff decided that a more experienced player such as Cilic would give them their best shot in pressure moments. Boy, were they right even though mentally Cilic had suffered the two previously mentioned loses. While he is not "a doubles specialist," it did not matter at all. We were reminded that good tennis players are good tennis players whether playing doubles or singles. When the pressure is on, they perform. If a doubles team comes out with the right game plan, it makes all the difference in the world. Unfortunately, for the Bryan Brothers and all the cheering American supporters, that fact was made apparent that day.

The match started with the Croatians stunning the crowd by winning the first set 6-2. The Bryan Brothers came back in the second winning 6-2, and the crowd was feeling better. However, the Croatians amazingly won the next two sets 6-2, 6-4.

The result itself was somewhat remarkable. The home team, with arguably the most successful doubles team of all time, was not able to pull it out. The victory by the Croatian doubles team fueled the momentum for Cilic to beat Isner and Coric to beat Sock in singles the next day and earn the Croatian Davis Cup team a 3-2 overall win.

While most of the coaches knew, for the previous reasons mentioned, that the Croatians had a good shot at beating the Bryan Brothers, what was more interesting was the specific play being used over and over by the Croatians against the US team. It was probably one of the more educational moments for us in our years of watching and observing pro doubles play. In a way, it was very simple. The Croatians pre-planned a strategy based on their strengths as players.

Here's how it worked. Marin Cilic has very piercing and solid groundstrokes. As we said before good tennis players are good tennis players whether they are playing singles or doubles. Besides, Dodig is incredible at the net with both his hands and his efficiency of movement when poaching. With these two strengths in mind, they created a strategy that worked beautifully especially when Cilic was serving on the ad side. The Bryan Brothers never figured out a good counter. The Croatians were ready and fired up to use their strategy.

Here was the Croatians' play. Cilic would serve out wide to Mike Bryan, which was to his one-handed backhand being a right-handed player. Instead of being in "regular doubles formation" the Croatian team was in Australian doubles formation when the server and the server's partner are on the same side of the court. Why would this help them? Since Cilic and Dodig were both on the ad side, Mike was forced to hit to where Cilic would then move over and rip his forehand or Dodig was able to poach and put the return away. The one time the US did win a point Mike had to rip a ball very deep and aggressively down the line. However, Cilic was serving the ball consistently deep in the service box which made it hard for Mike to do that.

Watching this reminded us of the advantages of using strategic doubles patterns to help succeed in doubles. We will now briefly discuss this pattern as well as others and how they can be used.

Australian Formation- As we discussed in the story above, this formation can be used effectively when you are trying to take away a certain strength of your opponent. In the Davis Cup example, the Croatian team removed the Bryan Brothers' ability to use a good crosscourt return on the ad side.

This also works well if the server's game is not *serve and volley*. As in the Davis Cup example, it allows a server if he/she has a big forehand to hit that shot or a good volley player at the net to poach on the return if he/she sees the opportunity.

Both Back on the Return – Another effective formation in doubles, can be with both players back on the return. If you look at pro doubles matches, sometimes on the first serve both players (on return team) stay back. In fact, you will see the Bryan Brothers do this quite a bit in their doubles matches due to the speed of the serve and the effectiveness of the volley person at the net. We are only advocating this strategy if both your opponents have both strong serves and strong volley partners.

The "I Formation" – In today's game you will see either the straight I formation or the modified I, which is becoming more prevalent in the pros. This is a specific strategy based on the server being able to place his/her serve and the serving team knowing the weaknesses of the return game of the opposing team. If those two factors exist, then we suggest trying this formation. We certainly used it during our college tennis days. Besides being fun to use, it throws the other team off because they have no idea where the server's partner at the net is going.

Serve and Stay Back – The other formation that can be used is that the server serves and stays back. While we grew up not playing this style, there are benefits to it. Take Jack Sock for example. He is one of the best doubles and singles players in the world right now in terms of results. He currently is in the top 20 in both singles and doubles on ATP tour - #19 in singles and #14 in doubles (8/11/2018). He mostly serves and stays back on his serve in doubles and has been successful at it. He can rip his huge forehand after his serve.

Summary

Sure, conventional thinking is that doubles starts one up and one back and then serve and volley. We have seen many teams serve and volley for the sake of serve and volley but lose 6-0, 6-0 and not change their strategy just because serve and volley is "what you should do in doubles." While we prefer that strategy, and statistics shows that is the most successful one, it does not mean it is right for your team. Sometimes you must think outside the box and try other strategies that might help you be successful.

Five Essential Qualities of Doubles Poaching

"The biggest risk is not taking any risk...In a world that is changing really quickly, the only strategy that is guaranteed to fail is not taking risks."
Mark Zuckerburg

An aggressive mindset in poaching is important for a doubles player. In this chapter, we will discuss five essential qualities we see in doubles poaching. These include – **productive, optimal, accurate, communication, and high probability.**

Before we talk about these qualities, let's first define poaching. Poaching is when as the net player you move over to take a shot that is directed to your partner who is on the other side farther away from the net. So, knowing the qualities behind good poaching is essential. Here they are:

Productive – Being productive means, by making this move, you will put the other team in a defensive position where your team has a higher chance of winning the point.

Optimal – As the net player you want to be the person looking for the opportunity to help your partner who is serving. However, the word "help" here is critical. If you are going to move over to hit the ball, it must be done at the optimal time. This means that when poaching on the return from the opposing team, it benefits your team more for you to hit the return from the opposing team than your partner who just served.

Accurate – If you are deciding to make this move you want your poaching shot to be accurate and put the ball away or hit so deep that the opposing team's reply will set up the next put away shot by either your partner or you. If not, you are setting your team up to be in an awkward situation that the opposing team can exploit. Instead of being on offense you are now on defense.

Communication – Communication must be part of the process in doubles, which we cover in more detail in the next chapter. This is important because poaches are planned or unplanned. Either one can work very well. However, it is important that as a team you understand each one. The planned poach can be more effective because as a team you can plan out where the server is serving thus giving the server's partner a better chance of having a weak return to poach. One of the main factors regarding the unplanned poach involves determining whether the return from the opposing team is poachable or not. A poachable return generally means the return is one you can get to in one or two steps and hit above the net in a balanced, aggressive manner.

High Probability- Finally, once you have followed the previous steps you should have a high probability of knowing your poach will be successful. It does not have to work **100% of the time** but enough to help your team gain an advantage. While poaching is a great strategy, poaching all the time should not be done just for the sake of poaching. Otherwise, you might get burned down the line.

Summary

Poaching can be an excellent strategy for any doubles team, but it must be trained, practiced and executed correctly to be effective.

Top Ten Aspects of Doubles Communication

"Communication and communication strategy is not just part of the game - it is the game."
Oscar Munoz
CEO of United Airlines

In any relationship, including business, personal, social, friendships and marriages, communication is key. Of course, this is no revelation, so it should be no surprise to you that this same theory applies in doubles. In this chapter, we will examine the top ten communication aspects of successful doubles play that we feel will help all players, specifically juniors. We view each of these as equally important.

We will break them down into these four areas – **in the warm-up, between points, during points, and between changeovers.**

In the Warm-up:

Picking Sides – In the warmup, communicate which side each person will take to receive the serve. This gets you focused right away on how you are going to play the match. Usually the stronger returner and player overall takes the ad side since most game and break points are often played on this side, and they are crucial points.

Identify Any Weakness of Your Opponents – If you notice either player on the opposing team demonstrating an identifiable weakness during the warm-up, let your partner know immediately and strategize about it.

Between Points:

Always Positive Comments – Comments between you and your doubles' partner should never be negative. We know from our experience there is no value in telling your teammate who just missed a volley in the net, "Next time make sure you open your racquet more." Why is this? The reason is that your primary role in doubles after the point has been played, is to reinforce the other person's confidence. Thus, a negative critique does not reflect that approach but instead puts you in the role of the coach which is not your role. Instead say things such as "Great effort, or good try! We will get them next time." These words stress two things - appreciation for your teammate's effort and "we are in this together!" Never give technical comments to a teammate during a match—only after and usually only if your partner asks for tips for improvement.

Dual Positive Body Language – During all points, whether won or lost, both players need to exhibit positive body language such as shoulders back with good posture, or eyes focused on strings of their racquet, ball or opponents. Research has shown that body language and facial communication are 90% nonverbal. So, this means if you are frustrated that your partner missed a shot you might be showing the frustration without even saying a word and not realize it.

Specific Suggestions – When talking about strategies to pursue, be specific. This means for example if you suggest "let's hit our shots to the weaker player," suggest which player you think is the weaker one. This is okay because your suggestion is a strategic one and not technical.

Keep it Brief – The best doubles teams in the world either keep their suggestions very brief or use signals just like a pitcher/catcher communication in baseball right before the batter hits. As you develop your doubles' skills with accuracy of serve and return, signals will be more important. As you use signals, make sure you use these guidelines. The server's partner is the one who gives the signal in this order – where to serve and where the server's partner will move.

Pick up your Partner – This does not mean physically pick them up, unless they happened to fall on the court and wanted help. This means a mental pick up. Anytime your partner misses, be the person to cross the center line first and give them positive reinforcement. This is an important tactic the pros use all the time in doubles. Whether you have won or lost the point, some of the best doubles teams often fist bump or some other small touch with a simple encouraging comment after every point. In other words, don't just high five when you win the points.

Keep Communication Routines Consistent Regardless of the Score – Whatever process you have between points for talking about strategy keep that process regardless of the score. This means if you go back and go over strategy with your partner at the baseline, give a high five and run back to the net to get ready for the point then, do that every time.

During Points:

Simplicity Equals Efficiency – When calling a lob that goes up, the net person should say "mine" or "yours." If the lob goes over net person's head to the person hitting at the baseline, one of you should say "switch" or "stay."

Between Changeover:

Positive Team Oriented Comments – Phrases such as "Let's keep it up" or "Let's keep attacking the righty's backhand on our serves" is always a good strategy. These are positive, specific and team-oriented comments.

Summary

Just as *"location, location, location"* is important in real estate, *"communication, communication, communication"* is essential in doubles play. We hope these communication tips will help both you and your partner win your next match!

Point 6
Beyond the Court Life Skills

Transferable Life Skills – Part 1

Sancha Legg

The life skills that sport can teach us are well documented. Confidence, perseverance, leadership, and teamwork are usually high on the list. I believe tennis offers a few, sometimes subtler skills that can benefit future careers and don't get the attention they deserve. Here are the three skills I learned on the tennis court and that I practice daily when I go to work.

Life can be lonely

There will be moments in your career when it's just you. No boss to go to, no team to consult with, only you and your thoughts. Whether it is sitting outside a room waiting for your first job or sitting outside the boardroom before giving your head of department presentation, that seat can be a lonely place. The magic of tennis is that for a significant period of the time that you are on court you aren't physically hitting any tennis balls. That is a lot of time to spend alone with your thoughts.

I remember changing ends after winning a break of serve to go 5-4 up in the final set of an important match. All I wanted was to keep going with no interruption to keep the momentum. During the change over my head was full of everything that it shouldn't have been: Congratulating myself over the last shot, whom I might play in the next round, what my coach was going to say to me when he found out I won, what I was going to have for lunch. There was no one there to snap me out of my self-perpetuating line of thought, and I lost the final set 7-5. Tennis helped me in those moments when it's just you and those precious ninety seconds. Tennis helped me develop the ability to clear my head of all the noise, take deep breaths, remain focused only ever on the thing in front of you (in this case the next point) and most importantly repeat over and over again 'I can do this.' I would go on to lose many more matches, but I never feared those ninety seconds between games again. I embraced them. To this day, before any interview, or any presentation I imagine myself changing ends and go through the routine tennis gave me ending every time with 'you can do this.'

Play to your strengths but respect your weaknesses

Strong backhand? Weak second serve? Fitter than your opponent? You need to tune in to the next grand slam to realize every professional tennis player has strengths and weaknesses. While with some team sports you are positioned to play to your strengths. The kid who is fast is the wide receiver, the one with the strong arm is the QB. Tennis demands that you spend time on your weakness. You won't win many games without being able to put down a second serve! There are things we are good at that we don't realize or appreciate the value of at the time. Tennis taught me to be holistic and fair in thinking about myself. In my career, I think about how I can contribute to my job. I don't get hung up on just trying to be like the person ahead of me. I spend a significant amount of time making my strengths into real differentiators, but I allocate time to bring my weaknesses up to par. In tennis, I had a strong first serve because I was tall. My backhand has always been my weakest shot. In my career, I am very good at building client relationships, but I am less good at communicating with my bosses. I can't win tennis matches without a backhand, and I can't get promoted without the ability to communicate my successes. Tennis taught me to use my time wisely. My serve got better, and my backhand got satisfactory. I could have slowed myself down spending a lot of time and energy being what I was not ... the best backhand in town.

Deferred gratification is a virtue

It is a well-documented view that the advancement of technology and the birth of social media has led to an expectancy of instant gratification in many aspects of our lives. I believe that playing sport reminds us that true gratification comes when hard work pays off. The time, effort, investment, and support needed to become a complete player is the same prerequisites to become a complete boss. Technology can never replicate the fruits of that labor. Like you can't wake up tomorrow and be a Wimbledon champion, you can't wake up tomorrow and be at the top of your career. Tennis taught me that the road to gratification is a long one that must be respected. No shortcuts can be taken.

I remember being 11 years old and playing in the U12s division at a local tournament. The U18 girls' semifinal was going on at the same time. The older girls got to play on the grass show court and had an umpire. My match was on the hard court by the parking lot. I remember being in awe of everything about that U18 girl's match. The showmanship, the audience, how powerful the two girls looked. Fast forward six years and I am walking out on that court. 'Miss Bainton to serve' the umpire announced, and there it was, complete and utter unparalleled gratification.

Tennis is a complete sport. Without it, I would not be where I am today. The older I get, the more skills I can identify as being born out of my days on the tennis court. So, if all those hours of training and competing do not lead you to the trophy you always dreamt of, rest assured that the skills you have developed out there on that court will stay with you for life and be the building blocks for the career trophy you haven't even dreamt of yet.

Sancha Legg Bio
Sancha is former top junior tennis player in the United Kingdom. She is now Executive Director – Equity Sales - at Goldman Sachs. She is a board member of the England & Wales Cricket Board (ECB) Participation and Growth Board. She is a contributor to the Women's Tennis Coaching Association (WTCA) and holds a degree from the London School of Economics and Political Science (LSE).

Transferable Life Skills – Part 2

David Carl

It's hard to think about my childhood without including tennis. Everyone in my family plays, so as the youngest of two I got all my brother's "hand-me-downs" (those that were not destroyed by clay and body odor). We played on vacation, we played on junior high school courts, we played on grass, we played on clay, we played at the White House in 1990. We played wherever we could find a court with easy access and not too much water damage.

Mostly we played at country clubs. Northwood in Dallas was the first, and to a 6-year-old with a racquet, it was a tennis wonderland. Not only were there more courts than I could count, but the woods around the courts were ideal for chasing squirrels while I waited for nine-year-old Jeremy to finish off another octogenarian challenger. Jeremy was impressive at an early age.

I want to set the record straight. I have never defeated Jeremy. The only variable in this game is how brutally he annihilated me, and how much he would laugh when I threw fits. Jeremy had a very disarming trait of laughing whenever an opponent threw his racquet or yelled terrible things. In Jeremy's defense, tennis-cursing is quite funny. "Move your feet you *$%^$ing *$^&$!" "Go down the line you *&*(&ing *&*hole!" "Of course, he lobbed it over your head you net-hugging &**$$ $%^&!bag!" People wearing all white and screaming at the heavens wielding a cat-gut frying pan is impossible to take seriously. So, you really can't blame Jeremy for laughing, and magically his opponent would usually laugh too, and stop acting like a baby. Yes, frequently the petulant opponent was me.

When Jeremy was young, I remember that he looked up to Ivan Lendl and Pete Sampras: level-headed players who kept their cool and never over-celebrated or over-criticized. He would have LOVED Federer as a kid. I'm sure of it. On the other hand, I was more of an Agassi guy. He was fun! I just wanted to hit the ball hard enough to put a smoke-filled hole in my opponent's racquet. And I wanted to beat my brother. Just once! But Jeremy's consistency was stultifying. I know he must have missed a few shots in those years, but I have no memory of it.

I was also blessed and cursed with a blistering forehand. When you are 7 years old, and a crowd of old guys stops to watch your forehand and fills your head with comments like "that kid's a natural," "I've never seen anything like that," and "he could play on the tour with that forehand," ...it messes with you a little bit. Everyone who saw me play at that age would gush about my forehand, and it was a lot of fun to hit! The occasional point I would win against my brother was a forehand down the line that he couldn't reach, or I'd hit it with so much topspin that he was sure it was going out, but it dropped in like Nadal's amazing groundstrokes.

However, with all this natural talent and my desire to be Nick Bollettieri's next protégé, I didn't like practicing very much. To be fair I was already practicing piano, Tae Kwon Do karate, gymnastics, and baseball like any good suburban boy from Dallas in the 1980s. But if I loved winning at tennis enough, I would have practiced my toss for hours until it was the perfect height for the perfect serve. I would have drilled more and gone to more tennis camps and let the rest of my game catch up with my fantastic forehand. Even though I played competitively for six years, I never really loved winning tennis matches enough to do the extra work. I wanted to have a life outside of tennis, and do other things like camping, playing with friends and theater. I did love tennis, but not in the way **you must love it** to do it as a career.

I love getting out there and playing, and I still love doubles way more than singles because it feels like a fun social event more than a serious solo event. If I'm honest, I probably only play a couple of times a year now, and usually, it's with my brother or my Dad. However, I like knowing that I can play whenever I want, and if I ever want to pick it up again, there's not that much dust to brush off. Anyone reading this book has probably heard that tennis is one of the few true lifetime sports, and I look forward to playing again when I'm older.

But wait a minute, that can't be it! I can't just write a chapter about how I had this great forehand, burned out, and then barely play anymore. That's almost sad. That can't be the end of the story!

It's not.

I probably should have mentioned that I'm an actor, impressionist, writer and solo performer living in New York. At 16 I "got the bug" and haven't been able to shake it for 22 years (do the math). In the past four years, I've taken 2 of my solo comedy shows to 2 continents and eight states for over 100 performances. I've recorded dozens of voice-overs for radio, TV, film, and the internet. I've appeared in movies and television (www.davidcarlonline.com). The one thing that all those experiences have in common is something I learned on the tennis court: **confidence**.

I started tennis at such an early age that it's hard to say if my confidence came first, or playing tennis brought on my confidence, but I'm happy to give this point to tennis since I'm not sure.

When you play tennis, you must stand alone in the middle of a giant court and face your opponent with either no one watching, or your parents, or your coach, or sometimes a crowd. They will see every mistake. They will see every emotion. You are exposed, and if you play longer than a couple of times, it is something you just must get used to. You also must get used to the idea (even in doubles) that no one is there to help you. No one can get to that drop shot or run down that lob. No one can hit your serve or return one for you. No one can practice for you, and no one can win for you. More than anything else, I learned how to trust myself. I learned that even when you are on a team, there are many moments when you must dig down and be self-sufficient.

In my line of work, you must have the same mindset. I'm a freelancer, and most of what I do involves doing every part of the job...not just the acting which its own barrel of worms. Let's take my solo shows for example. I rarely get to show up and do it for a full house and call it a day. Usually I must make programs, send out press releases, communicate with venues, communicate with my director, communicate with my producers, repair props, buy new props, wash my costume, bake brownies for the audience (don't have to, but why not?), do the show, clean up after the show, and start it all over again. Bottom line: if I don't do it, it won't get done.

Tennis is a complete sport. As a player, you *must* be a complete player because you *must* do every step. It's like being any kind of freelancer because YOU must do all of it. With tennis, you're the fullback, the safety, the linebacker, the center and the quarterback, and you're even the coach. You're even the defensive coordinator and the water boy. You're the whole show when you play tennis!

When I walk on set, I must not only know what I'm doing, but I must look like I know what I'm doing. I'm like a plumber. If you hire plumbers and they look like they don't know what they're doing you are going to be nervous the entire time they are in your house. Even if they fix the problem you'll probably be nervous they didn't and never hire them again. If they don't know what they are doing, then your pipes will explode, your house will stink, and you'll never hire them again. There is nothing you can do to make your plumbers better. They are either good at their job, or they aren't, and you must trust them when they say they can do it.

The same is true of acting. I must look like I know what I'm doing and be able to do it. There isn't time for a director or anyone else to help me through it. I must be able to do it. So, whether I'm playing a singing donut on **Blue Bloods**, a mover on **HBO's** *Divorce* with Sarah Jessica Parker or recording a **Super Bowl** commercial for Pringles with clients in multiple cities and no way to know if they like it or not. I must have internal confidence that runs so deep it is externally visible, so deep that you can hear it in another city.

When I feel that kind of confidence on set, sometimes I think back to where it all started...standing alone on a big green court...and that makes me smile, and I do another take.

<u>David Carl Bio</u>
David Carl is an actor, impressionist, writer, solo performer, and younger brother to Jeremy who has never once let David win. David plays tennis now for fun, and for work has performed on TV, Film, stage, comedy clubs, in commercials, voiceovers, and has travelled the world with his comedic solo shows. The first stage he ever performed on was a tennis court.

Overcoming Adversity

"You always recognize great champions...how they came back from a loss."
George St.-Pierre
Canadian Mixed Martial Arts Champion

"For me losing a match isn't failure, it's research."
Billie Jean King

Tennis in its purest sense is about a player overcoming adversities to win a match. What are those adversities? They include wind, sun, cracks in the court, our opponent making bad line calls, an early morning match, playing several matches in one day, a language barrier between you and your opponent, and dealing with annoying opponents' parents, coaches or even teammates during matches to name a few examples. It also means adversity such as coming back from a major injury or having to get a new coach because the old coach moved.

    Before we look at specific tennis examples, let's look at several successful people in different facets of life outside of tennis who overcame adversities and were still successful in their field of endeavor.

    Albert Einstein, never spoke in the first three years of his life. Bill Gates' first company, Traf-O-Data, failed miserably. Although the exact number of tries has been debated, ranging from 1,000 to 10,000 attempts, it's safe to say Edison *failed* a great deal before he successfully created his beacon of light. What was his response to his repeated failures? *"I have not failed. I've just found 10,000 ways that won't work."* This information comes from this link https://www.huffingtonpost.com/2013/09/25/successful-people-obstacles_n_3964459.html.

    Coming back from injury – Sloane Stephens and Thomas Muster, both Grand Slam champions after coming back from injury, know about this. Sloane Stephens, before winning the US

Open in 2017, had been sidelined for 11 months after a foot injury and underwent surgery in January of 2017.

Thomas Muster had to hit groundstrokes in a specially designed chair to stay fit after his left knee was ruined in an accident in a parking lot at the 1989 Key Biscayne tournament. He returned six months later to win the 1995 French Open and briefly reach No. 1 in the ranking.

What can we learn from these stories? It's simple. The players mentioned here showed resiliency and never gave up. We would say they did a few main things in the process.

First, *they stayed focused* on what they loved, not the problems they were facing. It goes back a little to the conquerors' vs. complainers' theory. They certainly had a conquerors' attitude! Second, *they figured out ways they could still be actively working on skills* to keep them successful at their craft. Remember tennis players have three main components they can control – **mind, hands, and feet.** If one of those gets injured, hopefully, you can still work on one of them - the mind - if not two of them - mind plus one of the others. Think about what Muster did. He could not use his legs, but continually practiced with his hands (his swing) and his mind.

Having to get a new coach – If you are fortunate enough to have the same coach for your whole career, count your lucky stars. We both had various coaches growing up and still turned out as pretty good players. This happened despite us even living in the same area throughout our junior playing days. Most touring pros will say the same thing. We must first understand there is a high probability that you will have different coaches over which you have no control. When deciding on a new coach look for all the qualities we already discussed earlier in the book. The most important one is to make sure you feel a level of respect can be established between you and the coach. Without this, it is hard to experience the other qualities in this crucial relationship.

Finally, if you have established a level of respect with the coach and he/she can work with you in this order—person, athlete, and player—then keep an open mind to any suggestions the coach

may have about your game. However, if at any point you are not comfortable with a technique change or other change to your game then make sure the new coach knows that.
Summary

Tennis by its nature is about overcoming adversity. We have found that the principles for dealing with those adversities can be applied to life in general.

Goal Setting

"Obstacles are those frightening things that become visible when we take our eyes off our goals."
Henry Ford

Before we discuss goal setting, we would like to share a story about it that we feel illustrates the importance of it.

One of Jeremy's players was regularly playing USTA tournaments and was looking to crack the top 50 and higher from being around 90 to 100 in the USTA Mid-Atlantic Section. She was a very committed student coming to our program three times a week for our High-Performance classes. While she was committed to tennis, she also was equally involved in another sport.

After class one day, Jeremy was thinking there must be something we can do to get her tennis game going and tap her desire to improve her overall game if that is what she wants. Jeremy first took a harder look at what was going on in her tournament matches by asking the right questions of her and her parents about her match play. For example, questions such as "In what situations in her matches is she losing the most points?" and "Is she confident with her serve and return of serve?" Through this process, Jeremy found out that while she was doing well in the rallying aspect of the matches and when she came to the net, Jeremy started realizing she was lacking total confidence in her serve and specifically had no confidence in purposeful placement when she served. It made Jeremy realize that too many times in his coaching he had forgotten to focus on the shots that start the point for the player. For 12 and under she had a good forehand that she could direct but was not able to set it up with a good serve. In addition, Jeremy provided her and her parents a detailed development plan that focused on her serve first, and set goals that were agreed upon by Jeremy, the student, and the parents.

Because of taking the time to provide the developmental plan for her she decided to focus on tennis more. In the next three months, she won three tournaments. Also, Jeremy committed to coming to watch her tournaments including one of the ones she won. The parents so appreciated Jeremy taking time out of his day to come to watch and support her. Jeremy will never forget the parents saying it was not that she won but that they saw the commitment he had to focus on the specifics that would help her improve and in turn be more confident when playing tournaments. Her ranking improved to 40 in the USTA Mid-Atlantic.

With that story in mind, let's now go back to our thoughts about goal setting. While principles like **specific, measurable, achievable, relevant, time-based, effective and revisable** are important to goal setting, we also like to use the letters in GOAL to discuss goal setting using these four themes – **growth-oriented, organized, accountable, and longevity.**

Growth Oriented – The first part of goal setting means it must represent a *growth-oriented mindset* versus a *fixed mindset*. Dr. Carol Dweck, a researcher at Stanford University, describes these ideas in the following way. *Growth mindset* means people have the belief that their learning and intelligence can grow with time and experience. Dr. Dweck points out that growth mindset people tend to embrace challenges and be persistent in the face of setbacks. *Fixed mindset* means people believe their qualities are fixed traits, and they cannot change. We certainly believe that you must have *a growth mindset* to achieve your goals.

Organized – Once you have established that you are using a *growth mindset* to achieve these goals, next, you need to understand how the goals are organized. One of the critical things we have learned through working with juniors and the USTA High Performance program is proper periodization planning. This means that when you are setting out your developmental plan make sure it is organized where all the three major players—student, parent, and coach—know their roles. Also make sure that plans are laid out in a manner that allows you to understand what your short, mid-range and long-term goals entail. One thing we have learned from the USTA High Performance program is to include in your plan three areas of technical focus that correlate with and help you meet the goals and vision you have laid out for yourself. For example, one of Jeremy's high-performance players established in his long-term vision that he needed to improve *return of serve*, *serve consistency on second serve* and *groundstroke shot selection on defense*. So, the drills and training Jeremy and he did centered on these specific areas, prioritizing each one.

Also, make sure your plan does not include just *outcome goals* (ranking or results) but also *performance goals*. Performance goals focus on the skills that a player can perform and track. For example, if you are working on second serve consistency then set a goal of a specific second serve percentage during a match. As a long-term goal, set SMART incremental second serve percentages that can be reached over a particular time. We have often seen how some players are too heavily focused on outcome goals and therefore when those goals are not achieved the player views him/herself as failing. It is imperative when goal setting to ensure that performance goals are established before outcome goals.

As we learned in our USTA High Performance training, goal setting, whether short, medium or long term, should be done including tactical, technical, physical, and emotional goals. Achieving goals is great, but you need to know the steps to get there. Remember, a bad plan done well is still a bad plan.

Accountable - Once the goals are established with the right mindset and are organized, you need to ensure that you can hold yourself accountable to working as hard as possible to achieve them. This means you are 100% behind the goals you and your team has set. We have found this is a considerable part of goal planning, especially for juniors. The reality is coaches can help you come up with the greatest developmental plan possible. However, if you are not ready to be accountable to follow it, *then what good is the plan?* Remember as we have discussed before, the player must be the driver on this journey. The base commitment for the player's journey must come from the player first, not from the coach or the parent. Goals should be player-driven with guidance from the coach and encouragement by the parents.

Longevity – Finally, ensure that the goal-setting process is one you can continue to use for the long term. As you continue to improve your overall development, your goals will change, and you don't want to be reinventing the wheel. This ability to have a good goal setting process is important for life as well as tennis.

One way to achieve longevity with goal setting is just like a good business—you need to have a vision statement. A vision statement for business describes the organization as it would appear successful in the future. A tennis player can use the same concept. It simply means a player is establishing a vision for his or her game. We have found this very helpful in our tennis journeys. We are grateful for mentors along the way including parents, coaches and others who helped us understand and craft our vision statement for the journey. We wouldn't be where we are today if others hadn't helped us along the way.

Summary

Goal setting will always be a vital part of any journey—professional, educational, sports—but most importantly your life journey.

Point 7
Loving the Journey

Keys to Longevity

"If you can react the same way to winning and losing, that's a big accomplishment. That quality is important because it stays with you the rest of your life, and there's going to be a life after tennis that's a lot longer than your tennis life."
Chris Evert

Before we dive into this chapter, we want to touch on the overall point of "Loving the Journey." As we stated earlier, tennis is a journey. It started with patient and supportive parents and coaches who planted the seeds for our love for the game. We believe "loving the journey" is grounded in these three basic principles – **understanding the keys to longevity, keeping it fun and enjoying the moment.** These are the themes of the first three chapters in this section of the book.

We begin with *the keys to longevity* by examining our overall philosophy as coaches based on **Love it, Learn it and Live it,** a philosophy that drives everything we do in our interactions with the players. We will look at all three of them as they relate to the following phases of the tennis journey – **training, match day and post-match day.**

Love it – We both grew up loving training as players just starting out. As juniors, we even loved those early bird training sessions before school started. It all began with the seed of our love for the game watered and nourished by the encouragement of both parents and coaches. Think about a seed becoming a flower – **the player is the seed that continues to grow, the soil or the nourishment is the coach, and the water or encouragement is the parent.** Without all three we would not be in a position to write this book or coach tennis.

We also love match day! Even as adults we love playing high-level adult competition when we can. When we do get ready to play in adult league matches or tournaments, we use the same formula we used as juniors to prepare.

As we discussed earlier in our mindset chapter, we love reflecting on our matches and how we can improve even if playing competitively is something we don't do as much since we coach full time. It goes back to the way your brain learns a language. If you learn a language at a very young age, even if you don't speak it regularly later in life, you never really lose it. So, with tennis, we learned our love of the game early on, and we have never lost it and never will.

Learn it – We coach, write and research because we love what we do, and we always want to be better. As junior players, we had the same attitude. Between lessons, we both would read ***Tennis Magazine***, watch instructional videos of Ivan Lendl, John McEnroe, Jimmy Connors, Chris Evert, Steffi Graf and go to college tennis matches in our area with as much enthusiasm as attending a college football game.

We also would journal our journey growing up. Our best coaches always inspired us to understand the importance of journaling our matches and practices and what we learned from them, whether we won or lost. This has been extremely helpful in our coaching. Students relate better to stories, not lectures. So, any player wanting to be a coach later in life needs to realize the importance of this. We never viewed journaling as "busy work" but an enjoyable part of the process. Nowadays, players and coaches have access to many digital resources in this regard. If you are a high-level tournament player, this should be a vital and fun aspect of your journey.

Live it – Finally, we think we get better at living life because of the game of tennis, not because life makes us better at tennis. We mean by this that the tennis journey has taught us how to experience our life journey more fully. As we discussed in a previous chapter on transferable life skills in tennis, the values and skills you learn through tennis should correlate to helping you be a better person, whatever your passion in life may be.

Summary

All these principles come down to one thing – no one can force you to be happy playing tennis. In the end, it is up to you - **Love it, Learn it and Live it!**

Keeping it Fun

"The rewards are going to come, but my happiness is just loving the sport and having fun performing it."
Jackie Joyner Kersee

Keeping it fun is one of the most important parts of your tennis journey. In this chapter, we will discuss some ideas and tips for doing that. However, first let's remind ourselves of the benefits of youth sports, period. These benefits are divided into three areas: *physical, social and psychological*. The reason we mention this is that all the methods for keeping the sport of tennis fun must relate back to these three areas.

Why do kids play sports in the first place? Because they want to have fun! Yes, they also want to compete and to win and be part of a team, but ultimately the reason why anybody picks up a racquet for the first time is because the game of tennis looks fun. As we navigate the junior pathway, it is imperative that we remind players at any level that the reason they did it in the first place is because of the sheer enjoyment they get from playing tennis. When the sport creates stressors for you, and inevitably it will, don't lose sight of why you played it in the first place. Some focal points of how tennis can stay fun are:

Find Fun Playing Options Early – This can emerge in several forms. A couple that have been helpful to us and our players have been match play classes, USTA Junior Team Tennis or playing in entry-level tournaments.

One entry level tournament that can be super fun for 10 and under players and other age groups is USTA Tennis Bashes. We have held several at clubs where we coach, and they have been lots of fun for both kids and parents. Below are some of the main benefits of this type of event.

- **Provides a fun playing opportunity for kids**– One of the biggest joys we have had as coaches has been seeing that 90% of the players in our first Tennis Bash at a club where we both worked were from our program. It was great to see them have the opportunity to start the tournament playing process in such a fun way.

- **Helps kids learn how to play tennis and not just drill** – As coaches we have focused on coaching the game to turn our students into players of the game not just drillers on the court. Tennis Bashes ensure our coaching is much more efficient and effective to help kids get ready to experience the five basic situations in playing the sport which are: **rallying from the baseline, coming to the net, dealing with the opponent coming to net, serving, and returning.**

Participate in Family Events – Our own best memories early in our tennis careers are family related. Some of the first tournaments we both won were with our family members, Tim with his sister and Jeremy with his dad. We realize the dynamics of doing this for every family are different, but if it can be done in a fun atmosphere, then we suggest trying it. This can help keep the parent/child or sibling/sibling tennis relationship healthy.

Physical Fitness Benefits - It is a scientific fact that physical activity provides a multitude of health benefits and leaves the participant in a positive state of mind. Encouraging the fun of running, jumping, and playing instead of the mental attitude of "win or else" makes for a better and more enjoyable experience on the court.

Healthy and Fun Competition - This is an area of junior sports in general that gets destroyed by outside pressures. The reality is that if you remove the stress of the event, the parent and the coach, the competition of playing a match against someone else is a stimulating experience which includes trying to out-strategize your opponent, enjoying your excellent shots and reflecting positively on the misses. Congratulating your opponents instead of vilifying them when they hit a great shot is crucial to enjoying the experience. Try to let competition be fun and remain fun. There is no better example of this than Roger Federer and Rafael Nadal.

They clearly love playing and have the strength of character to enjoy both the wins and the losses. Neither one ever makes excuses because they embrace the art of competing.

Develop Friendships and Teammates - Tennis can be a lonely sport but having a core group of practice partners who are also friends is key to enjoying your time on the junior tennis journey. Also, it's fun getting to know students from other communities, cities, regions or countries. That is what is so great about tennis; it is a global sport, a multicultural melting pot of cultures that paints such a wonderful diverse landscape because of the people you will meet and have the chance to call friends and teammates.

You will also need people in your corner, people who are also on the same journey who can share both the highs and lows. It's clear that nobody can navigate the junior tennis journey alone! So be willing to share your experiences and reach out a hand to help others along the way.

Plan Rest and Recovery Time – Even if you are training to be on the pro level, planning rest and recovery time is important. While playing as much as possible can help you get better, it does not guarantee it. Rest and recovery time also help you keep losses in perspective instead of burning out.

Parents and Coaches Role - Parents and coaches, don't forget your role in promoting the fun aspects of the sport. Tennis should be fun for you also. Parents and coaches can enjoy tennis by simply being upbeat and excited despite the outcome; focusing on values and encouraging the child; consistently reinforcing praise for hard work and improvement; maintaining perspective for both you and your child, and lastly actually asking the question after every match or practice "did you have fun.

Summary

If fun is not part of both training and competing, you will miss out on the real joy that tennis has to offer you as a player and a person. If you do anything with your journey, keep it fun!

Enjoying the Moment

"You were born to be a player. You were meant to be here. This moment is yours."
Herb Brooks

This quote is from Herb Brooks, American hockey player and coach, who coached the American hockey team in 1980 to the gold medal beating the Soviet Union in an amazing upset. This quote highlights three things: *belief, the present*, and most of all *enjoying the moment*. In fact, the movie about this gold medal event is appropriately called "**Miracle**."

Earlier we mentioned players like Roger Federer being No. 1 at 36 or Jimmy Connor getting to the US Open Semifinals at age 39. As lovers of tennis history, we think these accomplishments are the result of one principle – **enjoying the moment.** From a winning perspective, both players have been and were very successful in their careers. That being the case, why would they still be playing with so much intensity later in their careers? We can't know for sure, but one reason is their **passion** for the game.

Our goal in this chapter is to show what we think passion means by discussing seven principles using letters from the word **PASSION—positive, accountable, sacrifice, satisfaction, introspective, overcome, and natural.**

Positive – Think about it. Why do we anything in life? We see it making a positive impact on our daily lives no matter the results. Not only that, we also see passion as something that allows us to make a positive impact on other people's lives.

Accountable – People who are passionate about something hold themselves accountable for the results. They don't look for scapegoats when missing a shot from lack of footwork or not focusing enough during a point. They don't blame others if they fail to take an opportunity in a match when they have it.

Sacrifice – People who are passionate understand sacrifice is part of the journey. They revel in the tough moments of the competition instead of shying away from it. They also understand that training to get to a high level takes sacrifice and dedication. In addition, sacrifice refers to an individual's commitment to the amount of education required to achieve high levels of professionalism.

Satisfaction – When players win a match, they have the satisfaction of knowing how they got there, not just the fact that they won. They appreciate all the little things that they had to do to be successful. This reminds us of the competitive mindset we discussed earlier in the book.

Introspective – They understand the importance of looking within first when setbacks, roadblocks or failure arise. They know that achieving great things in life comes from a player's inner drive first.

Overcome – They overcome obstacles and see them as part of the learning process.

Natural – While hard work and a growth mindset are important, much of what they do comes naturally to them. In the tough times of a match, it is the player's natural will and skill that helps him/her win.

Summary

Enjoying the moment is an integral part of the tennis journey, so we hope you enjoy every moment of your tennis journey!

WTA Player and Grand Slam Coach Offers Her Perspective

Sarah Jane Stone

We are excited to have Sarah Jane Stone, a former WTA professional player herself and CEO of the WTCA (Women's Tennis Coaching Association), contributing to this chapter. Here she highlights her journey as a junior player, a pro player and currently a pro-level coach. She shares her reflections on topics that we discuss in this book.

The trials and tribulations of junior tennis—nowadays those stories are the foundation of my life! Junior tennis is full of many highs and lows. So much is said about how difficult it is for parents to navigate, but seldom is there a mention of the struggles that teenagers go through, especially when it comes to player/coach relationships.

As the daughter of a former professional tennis player, turned WTA tour top 10 coach, I certainly had a few advantages over the other kids. Genetically, I was blessed with a lot of athletic ability and with one of the world's best coaches wholly invested in my career, you would think it was a dream come true.

My mum tells me I carried the racquet everywhere. They didn't let my brother start taking lessons until he was six, so when I wanted to go along too at age 3, they thought it was a little bit early. However, persistent nagging paid off in the end; so, they finally gave in to a very determined little girl, and off to tennis I went.

A once a week commitment evolved into a few times a week by the time I was 7 and my first singles title, the tennis school 15 and under event. Big win for a 7-year-old! I was clearly on the right track to achieve tennis stardom.

At this stage, I was having the time of my life when I was playing tennis. I loved hanging out with the other kids and banging the ball against the wall for hours on end while my parents ran a very successful tennis business at a prestigious Melbourne club.

Grace Park Tennis club played host to so many champions including Frank Sedgman, Margaret Court, Merve Rose, Pat Cash, and more recently Alicia Molik and Samantha Stosur. To this day, when I drive into the front entrance, I feel more at home when I head down to GP than anywhere else in the world.

When I wasn't at tennis I was doing athletics meets on weekends, playing cricket and football in the park and on a basketball team a few nights a week. I also spent three years doing karate which was very beneficial for my concentration. Even as a young girl I spent a lot of time daydreaming about the things I wanted to do one day, and karate was a tether for me.

I don't remember feeling this way, but somewhere along the line, I must have loved tennis. I woke up for every Grand Slam final Steffi Graf ever played in, wore her Adidas clothing line exclusively and made up a song with the line in it "You've got it that was Wimbledon right before your eyes."

However, one of the coaches who still works for my dad 35 years later reminds me of the times I would sit behind the light post and refuse to come out on the court and play. So, it wasn't all "happy days" when I was a kid growing up at the tennis club.

By the time I was ten years old, weekends solely consisted of playing state level junior tournaments. My parents took me everywhere, and at this time my dad was my primary coach. My results caught the eye of the state organization, and the national training group of Victoria invited me to practice. I loved it, and our practice venue was Melbourne Park, home of the Australian Open.

From about the age of 10, things started to get serious; my karate practice came to a grinding halt because we needed more time for tennis. Within the next two years, I had been a member of the state team, traveled on a national squad overseas without my parents and won the national hardcourt title.

Tennis was what I did. At training camps, the coaches frequently asked you what your goals were with most of the conversation always earnest. I would answer, "I want to be number one in the world." The trouble was I told the coaches what I thought they wanted to hear with a pit in my stomach because that was not my truth at all. Tennis to me was about having fun with my friends and getting to visit cool places. It never felt terrific to say that I wanted to be something that wasn't true to me, but I continued with the facade anyway.

Slowly but surely the fun side of tennis disappeared before my eyes. I had no control over it, and the most ironic part about it was that everyone around me believed I had so much talent that they honestly thought they were doing the best for me.

My biggest issue? I talked too much apparently. That's why I liked playing the sport because I wanted to have fun with my friends. I asked the coaches many questions because until this day I want to know why. Not to challenge; okay maybe sometimes I did as a young teenager, but I genuinely loved to learn. I wanted to know everything.

Coaching relationships can make or break a person's interest in the sport. When I was around 13 years old, I went to a national camp at the Australian Institute of Sport. I remember having a blast with the other campers. One day I was on the court with a coach that I didn't click with. He was a young coach from Canberra. I never really enjoyed being on his court. He had terrible energy and communicated in an egotistical and degrading manner, always belittling students with his sarcastic nature and the smirk on his face. Looking back, I'm sure I asked a lot of questions and might have been whispering in my friend's ear when he was addressing the group, but his way of "teaching me a lesson" was shocking.

A group of four girls was on his court, and I had just finished my turn at his four-ball feeding pattern. I was back by the baseline waiting for my next turn with the other two girls when he deliberately fed a deeper ball, so my friend Jenny would swing her racquet back to where I was standing. Mind you I was looking the other way, so I never saw her coming.

There was a loud crack as she has hit me on the side of the head with her forehand backswing. Immediately I bent over, put my head in my hands and started bawling my eyes out. The coach's response was, "that will teach you not to stand so close." That was it, not another word. For all he knew I could have had a severe concussion. At the very least that moment made me begin to look at the sport through a different lens.

Nevertheless, I persisted and put that troublesome 'lesson' behind me. Onwards to the Australian Junior Fed Cup team, more national titles and a general excellence scholarship at one of Melbourne's most excellent high schools, Wesley College. I spent my days balancing my increasingly demanding tennis schedule with my social life and academic commitment.

By the time I was 15, I had stopped working with my dad at least six times, attempting to work with other coaches he believed knew how to help me reach the professional ranks. He wanted me to be the best, but unfortunately, his way of pushing me through with the tough love method failed miserably; it NEVER inspired me to prove him wrong. Twenty years ago, athlete-centered coaching was for quack coaches who were reputed to know very little; typically, those professionals were not part of the old boys' club. Ironically those very coaches were the ones that were ahead of their time and are very much the norm today. The tricky thing about having a father who was one of the world's best coaches was no matter whom I worked with, he always knew more about the game than they did. Regardless of the potential of the working relationship, every new coaching relationship was destined to fail. Without realizing it or meaning to, my dad would undermine the other coaches when I told him what we had worked on in my last lesson. I knew he was right which made it hard for me to trust other coaches, let alone treat them with the respect they deserved.

The car ride home after a loss (practice or match) is one of the biggest nightmares in a junior player's life. It doesn't matter if their parent is a former Grand Slam champion or self-proclaimed armchair coach of the century, for the player the experience is pretty much the same. The public face of defeat goes away as soon as the car door closes, and the foot hits the gas. Coaches spend a lot of their time trying to instill the process-oriented approach into the player's psyche, but a parent can merely dismantle it in an instant.

After a loss (and sometimes a win) when emotions are running high, it becomes very personal to parents as they want their child to succeed so badly. So badly, in fact, they often lose their minds and become completely belligerent. Tennis monsters to be exact who suck every bit of light out of the junior player's tennis journey, leaving them frightened, confused, hurt, and miserable and desperately seeking approval. One solution that sounds relatively simple is that parents should only get angry if the player has a bad attitude. In theory, this makes sense, well not the getting mad part. However, it's sometimes the reason parents may feel the need to express their disappointment in their child's performance when they are making so many personal and financial sacrifices for the child to pursue their dreams. The problem is emotional parents will use the "attitude card" to justify explosive rage disguised as a poor attitude reprimand.

However, had the player won his/her match with a bad temper, most parents would overlook the behavior and celebrate the victory. I can assure you that those car rides home were some of the most horrible times of my young life. So, when I lost a tennis match, and my backhand sucked, I was still a young person of integrity who always put her best self forward. My dad getting so upset with me taught me one thing—to deal with disappointment or anger explosively, something that took quite a bit of unlearning as a young adult. Parents need to focus on the process and realize that, by reacting negatively to their child's losses, they are teaching them one thing—to be afraid of losing. This is often where *the result fixation* starts, and the enjoyment stops.

By the time I was 17, I had quit playing tennis three times. I've read back over my teenage journals noting the highs and lows of adolescent life. The highs, falling in love, making memories with friends and the occasional celebrity crush. The lows, oh so low, when you look back at entries hoping you don't have to play interclub on the weekend, you know something was very wrong. In reality, how wrong could it have been? At 15/16 I was once again playing for Australia on the junior Fed Cup team, touring all over the world with an ITF junior doubles ranking of world number 8 and singles 80. Despite all that success, I lived in fear of losing and having to deal with the aftermath.

At the time, of course, I didn't get why anyone would be angry at me if I wanted to hang out with my friends more than I wanted to practice. One of the most significant issues I have seen in my coaching life is parents wanting it more than the kids—this and coaches who don't get to know the player as a person and find out what makes that person tick.

When I head back to where I grew up, my closest friends are still the ones with whom I made those memories during my junior tennis days. It was indeed one of the most challenging times of my life and one of the most incredible ones. Many of us are still in tennis, and even those who are not, love heading to Melbourne once a year for the Australian Open.

Player-coach relationships can become lifelong friendships, and I now enjoy spending time with some of the players I have coached who are college graduates, even though they occasionally make me feel old. Colleagues have said to me over the years that coaches shouldn't become friends with their players, something that is not in alignment with my coaching philosophy. If I think about what could have kept me in the sport longer or the moments that I thoroughly enjoyed it was when I got to be myself on the court and felt like the coach was listening to me.

The ups and downs of junior tennis enabled me to have the experiences necessary to be where I am today, and even though another coach once deliberately flattened me in the end zone during a Frisbee football fitness session because I asked him one too many questions, I wouldn't trade my tennis life for anything.

It allowed me to establish a platform that is committed to changing the way coaches work with female players with much of the education relevant to coaching boys as well.

It was a conversation with one of my lifelong best friends that changed my path and now the way that women tennis players are taught across the sport. Nicole Kriz and I played junior tennis together, won a professional doubles title together and have spent many hours reflecting on our lives as tennis players. Over a bag of lollies, we recognized that the way coaches work with female players needed to change, so I went about forming the Women's Tennis Coaching Association (WTCA).

How can we be more impactful as coaches and how can we give each athlete the best tennis experience possible? It starts with communication. Adults quickly forget how difficult those teenage years were for them. Even though they were some of the best years of our lives, they were challenging to say the least.

Junior players need space to be themselves, to feel respected and have the trust and comfort to express their own opinions safely. We as coaches are asking them to buy into what we are saying, to trust us with their development. Inevitably, we need to be understanding and spend time building a relationship with them.

Here is the reality—kids will be kids; in fact, people will be people, and they are who they are. It sounds cliché, but it's the truth. Coach accordingly. Get to know players slowly, by building a rapport and allowing them to come to you. Being forceful seldom works. Be collaborative; let the student feel like part of the game plan. Coaches ask players to take ownership over their careers; however, they frequently spend training sessions telling them what to do rather than showing them and allowing them the opportunity to feel like it was their idea.

The basis of everything that we believe in at the WTCA is improved coach education to keep more girls in this fantastic sport that gives so much to so many. It's also true for boys. There are so many things that can lure young people away from tennis, especially when the environment is not enjoyable.

In 1994 one of my national coaches was a highly respected former professional player. He didn't get me as an individual at all. We had returned to practice after a three-week break from school, and I was so excited to see everyone. My friend Lia Di Mingo and I were having so much fun, chatting about what we did over the vacation, who likes whom and all sorts of nonsense. Coach yells out, "right Sarah and Lia, you can go home now." We looked at each other and smiled, cool we thought, we get to go home early tonight! But he was furious and angrily added: "all you two have done is talk all night so you can finish early and think about why you have wasted your time." We felt horrible; 5 seconds ago, we were so excited and enjoyed being at tennis, and we had no idea that we had been doing something wrong for the previous hour. We didn't even get the chance to correct our 13-year-old unprofessionalism; the first time we had been made aware that we were chatting too much was the moment we were getting sent home for the evening.

Two things were particularly wrong with the way that coach handled the situation: (1) one was he never said anything to us about saving the chitchat until after practice, and (2) he embarrassed both of us in front of our peers. Neither makes for a trustworthy relationship with a coach, and both certainly made us reassess how much we wanted to be part of the sport and his practice sessions.

In hindsight our coach was correct; we were talking while we were hitting balls. Nowadays as a coach, I have encountered how hard it can be hard when working with a group of kids, and a few of them keep talking. However, I handle it differently. I chat with the kids at breaks, allow them the opportunity to share with me and the other students. There have been times when I've needed to talk privately to one of them, but I always have been conscious of the fact that they should feel safe, cared for and allowed to be who they are. I recognized that they didn't have the experience to realize that they might be disrupting the group; after all, they were enjoying that moment in time.

As coaches we need to find ways to engage the students, finding ways to capture their attention. Be flexible. Cell phone addiction has become disruptive to humanity. Coaches, parents, juniors and professional players check their phones 100's of times per day. Should we ban phones from practice? Some coaches do; however, I don't see the need. I chose to lead by example; I don't check messages or make excuses to pick up my phone. I use break time to involve players in a conversation that I know is interesting to them. I can do this very quickly because over the duration of our coaching relationship I have taken the time to get to know each of them as a person. I know what their dog's name is and can ask them, by name, about their friends that they hang out with on weekends. As the old saying goes, players don't care how much you know until they know how much you care. Time and time again I have found this to be true. If you look around you will usually see that one coach whom everybody enjoys. Those are the coaches who treat their students with respect and know how to create a conducive training environment. They are not the coaches who say, "This is how I coach, so get used to it." Most coaches can work with a few personality types, but only a few coaches seem to be able to work with everybody. Be malleable.

Much of what I have talked about throughout this chapter pertains to the enjoyment factor which in turn retains students. Coaches must strive to make all students feel comfortable – comfortable to be themselves and accepted.

For some teenage girls, comfort can be hard to find. Looking back over those journals I came across a self-portrait - myself as a 15-year-old. I had managed to make a note of one or two positives, but my heart sank when I saw how many arrows were pointing toward perceived flaws, drastically outweighing the positives.

Body image is one of the hardest battles many women will fight over their lifetime, particularly during their teens. It's the endless quest to be perfect. Young girls are paying attention to the fact that their WTA role models are judged according to their outfits and how overweight or underweight they are. When asked about whom they are dating, fashion tastes and numerous other trash magazine topics that in no way speak to their ability as an athlete, it consequently affects the way young players look up to their idols. The message is you are not good enough the way you are, when in fact we were all born perfect.

Social pressure is unavoidable, but the way coaches talk negatively to girls (and boys) about their body image is entirely unnecessary. I have countless friends who were called fat by their male coaches and told to lose weight. Many were petrified of fitness assessments because they almost always included a skin fold test. I remember trying to keep my calorie intake to a minimum for the last few days before the test, just to make sure I passed the not too fat benchmark. I would routinely force myself to go to the toilet just before the calipers came out and I didn't drink any water until that part of the testing was complete. How is an athlete supposed to do fitness testing on two days of hardly eating and spending an entire day avoiding fluids? None of the coaches even considered the fact that having your fat pinched on your stomach in front of the whole training team might be slightly embarrassing. Even worse, it bred a competitive thinness environment that almost always harvests eating disorders. Fitness testing protocols have improved since the 1990's. However, the stats still show that eating disorders remain a significant issue with a study I remember reading stating that approximately 33% of female athletes suffer from eating-related disorders.

How can coaches broach the sensitive subject of maximizing athletic performance by maintaining an optimal body composition? If the coach has concluded that an athlete should alter her/his eating habits to lose body fat they should tread carefully. The WTCA baseline course suggests coaches start the conversation by using a safe approach. "What kind of foods do you like to eat?" Should the athlete rattle off a series of foods that are not ideal for performance, the coach can follow up with "are you open to some suggestions about food that might help you with your performance?" At this point, she may quickly shut the conversation down, and it will not always be by giving a verbal response. Coaches need to pay attention to her body language, and that anything but a yes is a no. This comes from the expert advice of elite performance sports psychologist, Dr. Michelle Cleere.

Young females deal with many awkward things, like getting their period for the first time or wearing a pad and being mortified about the chance that somebody could see it through their skirt. It's a tough time, and coaches who achieve the most success with girls in this age group are usually the ones that are highly emotionally intelligent. Real teachers are sensitive to other people's emotions and realize that telling a female player to get over it when she comes in crying after a relationship breakup is not only a waste of time, it can be damaging to the player-coach relationship.

If I could do it all again, I would pick tennis every single time. Those are the memories that I frequently revisit when I spend time with my tennis pals. The life lessons that I learned made me the person I am today. Adversity taught me the skills I would later rely on to sympathize with my players when they were going through similar experiences. Without the battling through times like dealing with a friend's drunken father trying to shake the fence down during our final set, I wouldn't have learned that two people can experience the same situation in a completely different way. It taught me a viewpoint other than my own, understanding that even though both of us were in it together on that day, our experiences at that moment were poles apart.

I know that my perception is mine alone and that I might see a situation from an entirely different perspective from that of the players I coach, and it doesn't make me wrong and them right or vice versa. Collaboration is the key to a successful coaching relationship; so too is the ability to recognize that both parties might be right (or completely wrong) and still be able to work together in finding the best way forward. Being a teacher has become my life. Serving others with integrity and compassion is something I look forward to doing every single day.

Sarah Jane Stone Bio

Sarah, originally from Australia, is a former WTA player who has competed in the main draw of Wimbledon and the Australian Open. She now serves as a world-class, professional touring coach. Sarah has coached, Samantha Stosur, who won 3 grand slam titles. Sarah is the Founder and the CEO of the Women's Tennis Coaching Association (WTCA). She has also served as the Director of Tennis at the Columbine Country Club in Colorado and coached at the University of Colorado.

For the Love of the Game!

Cristelle Grier Fox

This book is about loving the tennis journey. What I'd like to share are some of the key aspects of my journey from a personal decision to make Tennis MY SPORT, to family support, playing, competing, and then coaching others myself and some of my reflections on what helped me continue to love Tennis for the rest of my life. Here's a little outline of what I have in mind in this chapter.

1. My choice to make tennis number 1.
2. Finding a coach that instilled a love of work ethic with balance right between progress and winning.
3. Parents who always encouraged, reinforced values, supported.
4. A team that worked together towards a common goal and weren't best friends but best teammates.
5. Playing for something larger than myself.
6. My goal as a coach now is to instill a love of the game.

When I was 14 years old, I walked into my dad's office and declared that tennis was The Sport I wanted to concentrate on. I had played every sport available to me up until that stage: Track and Field, Netball, Tennis, Soccer, Kickboxing, Cross Country... the list goes on and on. I was a classic all-rounder, but something clicked in me that day, and my tennis journey began.

To this day, I attribute my continued love of tennis to the fact that I was able to make the decision, to make tennis my sole focus and desire, myself. I wanted it; it wasn't a projected desire from coaches, friends or family. As soon as I did make The Choice, however, friends, family, and coaches all leaped into gear, and the next several stages of my tennis journey can be attributed to them.

My dad found me a coach who instilled in me a love of working hard; of taking one step each day towards a larger goal. I was a talented, athletic young girl who hadn't yet learned how to dedicate myself to the pursuit of greatness in one area. My excitement, passion, and desire, coupled with the support from my family and coaches, meant that I caught up with the rest of my peers within a couple of years. Outside of my immediate support group, I had many people saying I had made my decision too late in life and that I wouldn't bridge the gap fast enough. What they hadn't accounted for, however, was my love of the game and my determination to be the best I could be. While my love of Tennis was expanding as I discovered new techniques, tactics, physical abilities, or other aspects of the sport, many of my peers were struggling with having played too much, too young—a decision they hadn't made or understood at the age of seven or eight.

I decided to make Tennis "The Sport," together with parents who supported me and taught me valuable life lessons and values. My coaches also encouraged me, taught me and found a balance between always working towards a larger goal while always concentrating on the here and now that enabled my tennis journey and allowed my love of the sport to blossom.

I always liked playing singles but had excelled at doubles. It wasn't until I started playing on the tour (having graduated from high school) that I realized why...I liked playing for something larger than myself. The tour though was all about the individual, and I had a hard time reconciling striving for greatness with it being all about me.

I realized that I had had my best results when playing with others on a team. I went to university in America, and that was when I found my place. I was playing for more than myself. I was playing for a team, a university, a shared common goal.

For every individual achievement I received, it was within the context of something larger. I had achieved them as part of a team, and I had worked for those achievements because of the team and the coaches.

I had spent the last ten years yearning for, fighting for and driving towards my tennis goals, but looking back, the only dream I'd had (besides wanting to win Wimbledon, of course) was to be the best I could be. There had been short-term goals, of course, but ultimately my end goal had been to be the best I could be, and I think that's an important distinction to have made. I wasn't driven by the ideals of fame or glory. I wasn't even driven by outside forces like family and coaches. Yes, they were there the entire time but as my support group, not my control group.

To find a passion in life is what we should all strive for; you can't have it shunted onto you. But then, once attained, the flames need stoking, and they need help and direction. Find mentors, teachers, friends and family who will help grow the love.

It wasn't until I started teaching that I was fully able to appreciate my competitive tennis journey and all those who helped me. I wasn't sure when my competitive journey was complete, whether I wanted to or would be any good at coaching. I had never taught before; though teaching other competitive tennis players came naturally to me (remember I had just finished my career myself), I didn't know I would have the knowledge or patience to teach someone who had never played before. It turns out that I don't mind who I teach. I love teaching the most basic things like how to grip the racquet. I love teaching the most intricate things, like what strategy to implement depending on where you are in the court, in the rally or in the match. My goal now is to use my passion, experience, and knowledge to help players love the game of tennis, and, once they've achieved that, to help them stoke the flames in the direction they want them to go. Love the game of tennis for itself, and it will take you on a truly magical journey!

Cristelle Grier Fox Bio
Cristelle grew up in London and played on the women's WTA Tour for a year before coming to the states to play college tennis. At Northwestern University she was ranked number one in singles and doubles in Division I tennis and was fortunate enough to finish her college career by winning the

2006 NCAA doubles tournament. From there she coached the Yale Women's tennis team for a year before working at Pond View Racquet Club in Westerly and at Mystic Indoor Tennis in Mystic, Connecticut. She then moved to North Kingstown in 2010. She is the North Kingstown Recreation Tennis Director.

Match Point

Final Thoughts

"When you do something best in life – you really don't want to give it up – and for me it's tennis.
Roger Federer

"Focus on the journey, not the destination. Joy is found not in finishing an activity but in doing it.
Greg Anderson

Our goal in this book has been to answer the question "What is the Complete Player?" Throughout the book, we have attempted to help you navigate your tennis journey. We can't do that for you. We laid out the principles, philosophies, and guidelines that helped us in our tennis journeys, and we believe they will help every one of you. We also hope that this book will encourage you to be more confident in your own philosophy as a player, whether you start out taking a summer camp as a five-year-old like Tim or hitting a Nerf ball with racquetball racquet strung up by your parents when you were 18 months old like Jeremy. Even if tennis is not your sport for life, we hope that it helps you find something you are best at it in life that you don't want to give up—something that makes you happy and others around you happy.

The greatest gift tennis can give is the ability to improve yourself positively—mentally, physically, emotionally, and socially— regardless of your age, gender or background. We hope that you are ready now to go out and enjoy the journey as you have never done before!

Glossary of Key Terms

You will find in this section key terms that we used throughout the book.

ABC's of Athletic Movement – Agility, Balance, and Coordination

Attacker – You are coming into the net from the baseline by choice and on balance for hitting the first shot at the net.

Australian formation in Doubles – Server and server's partner both start on the same side of the court with the server's partner at the net.

Coaching Tip – Sometimes only positive and is said without any real specificity.

Competitive Focus - Player understands the competition starts soon as soon as his/her feet step on the court.

Competitive Mindset - Winning is second to knowing you trained as well as you could and gave 100% mentally, physically, mentally and emotionally on the court.

Complete Player – A player who understands that environmental, technical, tactical, physical, and social components are equally important to having a successful, enjoyable and lasting tennis journey.

Elite Training for All Levels – Training that provides the physical, technical, tactical, and mental components to help the athlete perform at his/her very best level.

I-formation in Doubles – Server and server's partner both start very close to the center with server close to center mark and the server's partner close to the net over the center line crouched/kneeling down until the serve from the server lands in opposing team's service box.

Five Essential Qualities of Poaching - Productive, Optimal, Accurate, Cooperative, and High Probability

Five Phases of Tennis Play – Serving, Returning, You Coming to the Net, Opponent Coming to the Net, and Baseline to Baseline

Footwork Focus – Players move in such a way that they treat every ball like a "match ball," not a warmup ball during the warmup, then continue that focus on good footwork throughout the match.

Four Qualities of Goal Setting - Growth Oriented, Organized, Accountable, and Longevity.

GPS Strategy – A strategy based on these three main components – Geometry of the Court, Positive Mindset, and Using Your Strengths.

Mental Focus - Player focuses only on three things – him/herself, the opponent and the ball.

Modified I-formation in Doubles – Same as I-formation but server's partner is not directly over center but slightly shaded to one side or the other of the center line at the net.

Outlier Moments – Moments during a match where your opponent wins a few points, but you don't deviate from a tactical strategy that is working well overall.

Pivot Moments - Moments during a match where your opponent wins crucial points that warrant deviating from a tactical strategy that you have been using and cause you to create a new, more sustainable strategy.

Professional Coaching Guidance Tip - Both a positive and specific tip and one that has more of a mentorship role to it.

Reactor – You have been brought into the net in a manner that forces you into the frontcourt unbalanced.

S.M.A.R.T.E.R Goals – *Specific, Measurable, Achievable, Relevant, Time-Based, Effective and Revisable.*

Tennis Development Pathway Triangle – It includes three distinct sides: *Player, Coach, and Parent.*

Three Primary Ball Controls – Height, Depth and Direction.

True Grit Metrics – A system for evaluating how a player handles times in a match when your opponent is one game away from winning, and you are two or more games down. It specifically looks at ten attributes of positive body language.

Winning Only Mindset – A person who views success entirely on how much he/she wins.

5 S's of Training – Strength, Speed, Suppleness, Skill, and Stamina.

Made in the USA
Columbia, SC
01 October 2018